THE NEW Wood
Finishing
BOOK

THE NEW Wood Finishing

BOOK Completely Updated and Revised

MICHAEL DRESDNER

The Taunton Press

To Jane, Kaitlin, and Drew
DT
BS
KK

Cover photo: Scott Phillips
Back cover photos: Sandor Nagyszalanczy

The Taunton Press
Inspiration for hands-on living®

Printed in the United States of America
10 9 8 7 6

The Taunton Press, Inc., 63 South Main Street, PO Box 5506, Newtown, CT 06470-5506
e-mail: tp@taunton.com
Distributed by Publishers Group West

Library of Congress Cataloging-in-Publication Data

Dresdner, Michael M.
        The new wood finishing book / Michael Dresdner.
            p. cm.
        ISBN 1-56158-299-9
        1.Wood finishing. I. Title.
    TT325.D73   1999
    684'.084—dc21   99-13395
                            CIP

About Your Safety

Working with wood is inherently dangerous. Using hand or power tools improperly or ignoring safety practices can lead to permanent injury or even death. Don't try to perform operations you learn about here (or elsewhere) unless you're certain they are safe for you. If something about an operation doesn't feel right, don't do it. Look for another way. We want you to enjoy the craft, so please keep safety foremost in your mind whenever you're working with wood.

Acknowledgments

I am grateful to *American Woodworker* magazine for permission to adapt material that first appeared in their pages, to *Fine Woodworking* magazine for the use of sketches and photos that first appeared in their pages, and to ITW DeVilbiss Company for permission to reprint one of the charts from their excellent catalogs.

And a big thank you to all the folks who helped me with guidance, support, information, wood, samples, and a working computer, including, but not limited to: Chris Minick; Sandor Nagyszalanczy; Kevin Hancock; John Brock; Paul, Chris, and Ken Warmoth; Jeff Jewitt; Teri Masaschi; Jonathan Kemp; Bud Kersey; Gary Schwebemeyer; Ian Agrell; and, most especially, Jane McKittrick.

Contents

Introduction 1

Choosing a Finish 2
What Is a Finish? 2
How Finishes Work 3
How to Choose the Right Finish 8

Tools of the Trade 20
Safety Equipment 20
Application Tools 22
Other Tools 37

Stripping 43
Which Method to Use? 43
Choosing a Stripper 44
Taking It Off 51
Removing Old Stain 58

Preparing the Wood 62
Fixing Dents and Gouges 62
Sanding 66
Raising the Grain 75

Coloring Wood 77
What Is Stain? 77
Commercial Stains 83
Specialty Stains 84

Sealer, Primer, and Filler 101

Sealer 102

Primer 106

Pore Filler 109

Applying the Finish 117

Where to Finish 117

When to Finish 121

Applying Finishes by Rag 123

Applying Finishes by Brush
or Paint Pad 128

Applying Finishes by Spray Gun 132

Repairing Damage 146

Removing Excess Materials 146

Filling Voids 150

Touchup 155

Rubbing Out the Finish 160

What Is Rubbing? 161

Rubbing and Polishing Materials 166

For a Satin Finish 167

For a Gloss Finish 170

Machine Polishing 173

Resources 175

Glossary 176

Index 180

Introduction

I know. You hate finishing. You'd really rather be cutting wood. But you want the stuff you make to last, so it needs a finish on it.

The problem is deciding which one and how to use it. There's a wealth of different sandpapers, stains, brushes, spray guns, lacquers, varnishes, and even paint removers. It's really quite overwhelming.

But help is here. Within these pages you'll find up-to-date information on all that and more. From the very first step of how to choose the right finish, I'll take you through stripping, sanding, staining, topcoating, finish repairs, and on to the final polishing. Along the way, I'll guide you on what to buy and how to use it, and offer warnings and advice that can make the difference between a great finishing job and a nightmare. To keep it interesting, I've added a sprinkling of "finishing tales" and a good dose of questions—with their answers—from other woodworkers just like you.

It's all in here, clearly and simply explained, with lots of photos and drawings to assist when words alone are not enough.

Go ahead and take a stab at it. There's plenty of information in these pages to walk you through the hard parts and get you out of jams when things don't go right. I wish I could be there to help you in person, but I can't. This book is the next best thing.

So take a deep breath, relax, and dive in. You'll do just fine.

Choosing a Finish

Daydreaming is a favorite occupation for most twelve-year-olds, so I was probably in good company the afternoon I sat alone at my desk gazing at the side of my dresser. The problem was that while my mind had been on sabbatical, my hands had been busy: there, like a series of white scars scratched into the dark finish of the dresser, were my initials. "Did I do that?" I thought in horror as my attention snapped back to the present. Like most adolescents, I knew nothing of finishing, but my natural instinct for self-preservation kicked in as I spied a can of hair spray. "It can't get any worse," I reasoned as I sprayed and wiped the oily aerosol across the scratches. The gods must have been with me; I was elated as the white marks blended back into the color of the surrounding wood.

It wasn't a perfect fix, but the scratches were barely noticeable.

And so, like most woodworkers, I started my finishing career using what was available—a simple oil finish. In that case, my choices were limited to the confines of my room. But since then I have met all too many adult woodworkers who face their first finishing decisions with the same fear and confusion that accompanied mine.

All that is about to change.

What Is a Finish?

Like a good friend, a finish is defined not so much by how it looks, but by what it does. A wood finish can *protect* wood from scratches, dirt, stains, and wear; *enhance* wood's natural beauty, color, figure patterns, grain, and depth; *preserve*

wood from water, oxidation, and the sun's ultraviolet rays; and totally *change* wood's appearance by adding color and hiding defects.

A finish is a liquid, paste, or gel that can be spread thinly onto wood and will dry to a solid film. It may contain solvent to make it thinner and easier to work. The solvent will evaporate and disappear as the finish cures. The finish may also contain color.

One thing finish will definitely contain is resin. Resin is the glue or "binder" that stays behind on the wood to make the clear film we call finish. The type of resin is responsible for the hardness, flexibility, and resistance to stains, solvents, and water. For that reason, many finishes are defined by the resin they contain, such as nitrocellulose lacquer, polyurethane varnish, or shellac. Others have more

ambiguous names, like Danish oil or spar varnish. These are all defined later in this chapter (see pp. 8-18).

How Finishes Work

The way a finish turns from a liquid to a solid tells us a lot about how we should apply it and how it will hold up over time. There are two primary ways the finish turns to a solid: through evaporation or through a chemical reaction (and sometimes through both). For this reason, we divide finishes into evaporative and reactive groups.

Evaporative finishes cure when the solvent in them evaporates. The molecules of finish stay the same as they were in liquid form; only the solvent vanishes. Typically, evaporative finishes contain around 70% solvent, so when a coat of

What's in the can? Product names and advertising claims can be confusing if you don't understand the characteristics of the various finish types.

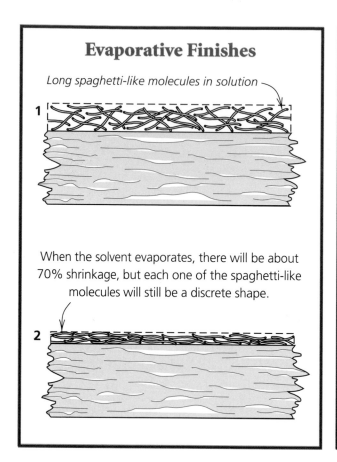

Evaporative Finishes

Long spaghetti-like molecules in solution

1

When the solvent evaporates, there will be about 70% shrinkage, but each one of the spaghetti-like molecules will still be a discrete shape.

2

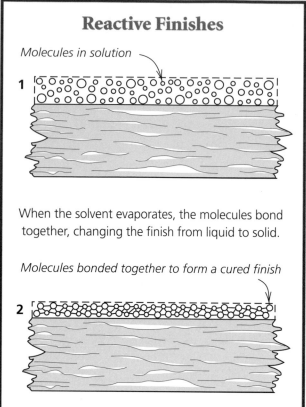

Reactive Finishes

Molecules in solution

1

When the solvent evaporates, the molecules bond together, changing the finish from liquid to solid.

Molecules bonded together to form a cured finish

2

Finish Characteristics

Evaporative Finishes (shellac, lacquer, wax, waterborne lacquer)	Reactive Finishes (oil, varnish, Danish oil, precatalyzed lacquer, two-part finishes: catalyzed lacquer, conversion varnish, two-part waterborne)
Contain large amounts of solvent	May or may not contain solvent
Dry much thinner than they were applied	Some dry without shrinking, some shrink
Will redissolve with their original solvent	Will not dissolve in their original solvent when cured
Do not require sanding between coats	Must be sanded between coats for good adhesion
Have poor heat resistance	Have good heat resistance
Will not show layers when rubbed or sanded	Will show layers if rubbed or sanded through two coats

finish dries, it is much thinner than when you applied it.

An evaporative finish will redissolve in its own solvent, which means it has limited solvent resistance. Each coat you apply redissolves the coats before it, so you don't need to sand between coats. If you buff and polish an evaporative finish, you will never get a visible line where you cut through one layer into a previous one.

Evaporative finishes are also called thermoplastic, or "heat flexible," because they will melt when they get hot. Thermoplastic finishes do not have very good heat resistance and are a poor choice for high-heat areas, such as kitchens and fireplace mantels.

Reactive finishes cure in a different way. As a reactive finish cures, its molecules combine into new, larger molecules that change it from a liquid to a solid. The resulting solid can no longer be dissolved by the original solvent, so the film tends to have good solvent resistance. For example, mineral spirits will thin out varnish, but once the varnish cures, mineral spirits will not redissolve it. Therefore, it is best to lightly sand each dried coat of reactive finish before you apply another coat. The sanding scratches increase the surface area, making it easier for the next coat to stick (see the drawing at right). Be careful, though—if you sand or rub through one layer into the layer below, you might see a line where the two coats meet.

Most reactive finishes are highly resistant to heat and a variety of chemicals, including alcohol. They are a good choice for kitchens, dressing tables, and bar tops.

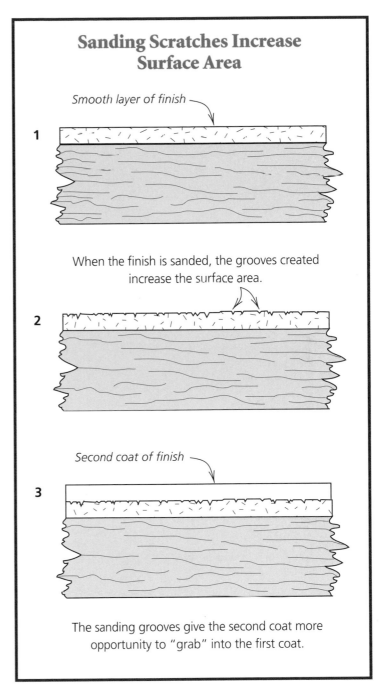

Sanding Scratches Increase Surface Area

1   *Smooth layer of finish*

When the finish is sanded, the grooves created increase the surface area.

2

3   *Second coat of finish*

The sanding grooves give the second coat more opportunity to "grab" into the first coat.

Safety

Finishing is no fun unless you can do it safely. Part of choosing the right finish is picking one you are comfortable with in your work environment. The three dangers you should be most aware of are fire, explosion, and biological hazards. How can you tell if a solvent is dangerous, very flammable, or highly explosive? Every finish manufacturer is required to issue a material safety data sheet (MSDS) for every product, and most manufacturers will send you a copy if you request it. On the MSDS you will find a wealth of information about the material, including any hazardous substances in it, the suggested exposure limits, the flash point of any solvents, safe handling practices, protective gear needed, and even what to do in case of a spill. These data sheets are not always easy to decipher, but they are getting better. Some of the more obscure acronyms on the MSDS, like TLV (threshold limit value), are explained in the Glossary on pp. 176-179.

Fire

Probably the greatest danger from finish solvents is the most immediate one: fire. Most of the thinners used in solvent coatings will ignite at fairly low temperatures, so it is important to keep your work area free of sparks or open flames. It is also a good idea to avoid exposed heating elements, like those found on inexpensive portable electric heaters. Even though they don't spark or flame, they are hot enough to bring the solvent fumes to their auto-ignition point (the temperature at which they will ignite without a spark).

Working with drying oils, like boiled linseed oil, requires special precautions. Oil-soaked rags or paper towels in a pile can result in "spontaneous combustion." That means the rags can burst into flame with no outside spark, flame, or heat source near them. Either incinerate oily rags immediately or lay them out one layer thick on a table edge, clothesline, or even the rim of your trash can. That way they can dry without generating heat. Once they are dry and stiff, usually overnight, they are landfill-safe and can be put out with the trash. Several years ago, a fire in a Philadelphia high-rise was traced to linseed-oil-soaked rags that a refinishing crew had left piled in a closet. The fire raged for 19 hours, did millions of dollars of damage, and left three firefighters dead. It took less than 5 hours for the rags to start the blaze.

Explosion

With some solvents, explosion is a threat. The smallest concentration of solvent fumes in air that can cause an explosion is called the lower explosive limit (LEL). Good ventilation is the key to avoiding reaching the LEL. As you design the airflow in your finishing area, bear in mind that most solvent fumes are heavier than air, so they tend to collect at ground level. If the floor is wood or wood over a plaster ceiling, think about what is below you. Fumes can easily pass through the floor and get trapped in the basement below, waiting to surprise anyone who walks in and throws an electrical switch or lights a match. Fume concentrations should be a particular concern if your furnace is below your work area; furnaces kick on automatically.

Biological hazards

Less immediate, but still important, is the way solvents affect us biologically. Individuals react differently to chemicals. Some people react violently to certain materials that others barely notice. It goes without saying that if a solvent or finish bothers you, avoid it. There are plenty of other options in these pages so that you can enjoy finishing without discomfort. But even when you don't notice it, certain solvents can have a deleterious effect on your health.

Oily rags left in the shop are a fire hazard. Let them dry by hanging them out one layer thick, and then dispose of them.

Luckily, most of the materials we come in contact with are quite safe. Even those that are more dangerous usually cause trouble only in large cumulative doses and pose little worry for the occasional finisher or hobbyist. Still, it is a good idea to wear protective gear— gloves for solvents that enter through the skin, respirators for solvents that enter through the lungs, and goggles for anything that is likely to hurt your eyes.

How to Choose the Right Finish

It is tempting to choose a finish based on what wood you are finishing instead of on how the finished piece will be used or abused. That is like choosing what you wear based on color alone, and not by whether it fits or how cold it is outside. With very few exceptions, any finish will go on any wood. The important issue is how you expect the finish to perform once it is on the wood. I determine that by asking three simple questions:

• *What must it endure?* Will it be on a bar top subjected to lots of spills, dents, heat, and scratches or on an art turning that is handled only occasionally and carefully? A deck chair needs a flexible finish to ride out wood movement from weather changes, a mantel needs to resist heat, a vanity is subjected to nail-polish remover spills, and children's toys should be nontoxic.

Now that I've made a new table for the kitchen, I want to put a good finish on it. We have kids, and we all tend to be kind of rough on it. I want a finish that will hold up under this abuse. What should I use?

Polyurethane, if you plan to brush on the finish, and catalyzed lacquer or conversion varnish if you prefer a sprayed finish.

To get the extra durability you need, use at least three coats of either of these finishes, sanding between coats. Ideally, you want the finish to be about 0.006 in. (six thousandths of an inch), or about the thickness of two pieces of standard typing paper. I know that doesn't sound like much, but for a finish, that's a lot.

• *How do I want to apply it?* Some finishes, like shellac, can be applied any way you choose, but others do best through a spray gun, on a rag, or with a brush. Certain coatings are flammable or give off strong odors that require heavy ventilation, while others can be used in the kitchen or the baby's room.

• *What should it look like?* Gloss or satin, colored or water clear, deep and glassy, or barely there? How thick you apply a finish affects its appearance, but some finishes do sport a certain look.

Once you've decided what characteristics you want, match them up with the appropriate finish. Below, in alphabetical order, is a series of thumbnail sketches of each finish that will tell you how each will perform, look, and apply.

Catalyzed Lacquer/Conversion Varnish/Precatalyzed Lacquer

Durability: excellent stain, heat, scratch, water, and solvent resistance
Apply with: spray gun
Solvent: special lacquer thinner, MEK (methylethylketone)

The terms catalyzed lacquer and conversion varnish are used interchangeably for a variety of very durable two-part spray finishes. Prior to spraying you must mix in a small amount of acid. However, you can get precatalyzed lacquer with the acid already in it. The material sprays like lacquer, flows out nicely, and dries to the touch in 10 minutes or so. Over the next several weeks, the dry coating cures, becoming tougher and harder. The film can be clear to light amber and just slightly more gray than nitrocellulose lacquer or

Catalyzed lacquer/conversion varnish/precatalyzed lacquer

Danish oil

shellac. It is perfect for very high-wear surfaces, such as bar tops, dining tables, and kitchens.

Danish Oil

Durability: poor water, scratch, and stain resistance, moderate solvent and heat resistance

Apply with: rag or brush

Solvent: mineral spirits, naphtha

Because it is so very easy to use, Danish oil is often the first finish we try. It is actually a very dilute, oily, amber-colored varnish designed to be applied and wiped off while still wet. The result is a very thin film that offers little in the way of protection but definitely enhances the beauty of wood, intensifying its richness and natural color. Each coat of Danish oil takes overnight to dry. Danish oil is good for

low-wear surfaces, like bookshelves and jewelry boxes, or where a natural "woody" appearance is more critical than durability.

Lacquer

Durability: very good water and stain resistance, moderate scratch and solvent resistance, poor heat resistance

Apply with: spray gun or brush

Solvent: lacquer thinner

Lacquer dries very fast, requires no sanding between coats, and results in a hard, brittle finish that easily rubs up to a high gloss. Depending on the resin it is made from, it varies from water clear (acrylic, CAB) to light amber (nitrocellulose). All have excellent clarity and enhance the beauty of wood. The brushable versions dry somewhat more slowly

Lacquer

Linseed oil/tung oil/walnut oil

I've seen the word "chatoyance" used several times on finishing chat rooms and message boards on the Internet. What does it mean and what does it have to do with finishes?

Chatoyance, from the French *chatoyer,* meaning "to shine like a cat's eyes," refers to the depth and shimmer that some woods exhibit under the right finish and lighting conditions.

The word was borrowed from the jewelry trade. Think of the semi-precious stone we call "tiger's eye" and how its colors flip back and forth from light to dark bands as you view it from different angles. Some woods do the same thing. If you have ever walked around a "ribbon" mahogany-figured tabletop in strong angled light, you'll have seen the ribbons alternate from dark to light. The same is true of some quartered woods, like "bearclaw" spruce, "tiger" oak, and figured maple.

Some finishes tend to enhance this effect more than others: We refer to that as finishing to bring out the chatoyance in the wood. Oils that tend to penetrate the wood, along with shellac, oil varnish, and to a lesser degree, lacquer, are all good candidates if you want to show off the wood's best face.

and are slightly less brittle. Lacquer is a good choice for moderate-wear surfaces, like living-room or bedroom furniture, where appearance is important.

Linseed Oil/Tung Oil/Walnut Oil

Durability: poor water, scratch, and stain resistance, moderate solvent and heat resistance
Apply with: rag or brush
Solvent: mineral spirits, naphtha

Oil sinks into wood and imparts a wonderful translucent shimmer known as "chatoyance." Each coat of oil takes at least one day to dry. Boiled linseed oil contains an additive to make it dry faster than raw linseed oil, but it still needs a day per coat. The most common application method is to flood it on then wipe it off. Oil makes a fairly soft and very flexible finish that tolerates dents without chipping. Most oils

FINISHING TALES

White-Glove Ladies

Out of earshot, we called him Jimmy the Hacker; although he was the senior finisher in the shop, he had a reputation for requiring two or three attempts to get a finish right. Still, when he was sober, he did some beautiful work, and the neophytes like myself enjoyed learning from this profane ex-marine in spite of his rather short temper.

One Friday, Jimmy was putting the finishing touches on a tabletop that had been keeping him busy all week. The finish was a fake-grained lacquer job with at least three separate color glazes used to mimic red oak. It was a bear of a finish to do, and this was Jimmy's second shot at it. His first effort was undone by a local flying insect. After the final coat of lacquer was applied,

a palmetto bug flew into the wet finish, and its death throes undid all of his fine efforts. You see, each coat of a lacquer finish redissolves all of the previous coats, so that the last coat again melts all others into one thick layer cake of translucent colors. That bug ruined the finish right down to the raw wood. There was nothing to do but strip the finish off and start over.

Now in its second incarnation, the table once again went into the booth for its final coat. Just as Jimmy wheeled the top out into the drying room, the shop's owner came by with two potential customers in tow—Southern matrons who still wore white gloves despite the eroding etiquette of the 1970s. The look of the still-wet lacquer under bright

lights must have been too much to resist, for as she walked past, one of the women gently ran her fingers across the glistening top. To her surprise, the lacquer moved aside, leaving a furrow down to the wood. It looked like the icing on a two-year-old's birthday cake after an unofficial tasting.

Those of us who saw the incident let out a collective gasp, convinced that we were about to witness the shop's first justifiable homicide. Jimmy turned beet red, and barely containing his fury, blurted out, "That finish is wet!"

"Oh, it's quite all right," replied the offender, holding up a clean, but now gloveless finger, "I had my gloves on."

are amber and will darken with age. It is an appropriate finish for low-wear objects, such as turnings or bookshelves, and especially areas of hand wear, like a railing or banister on a stairway. As the oil from your skin rubs constantly on an oiled wood surface, it actually builds it up and rejuvenates it. It is not a good idea to oil the insides of boxes or drawers, as the smell will linger for a long time.

Oil Varnish and Wiping Varnish

Durability: good water, scratch, stain, solvent, and heat resistance

Apply with: rag or brush

Solvent: minerals spirits, naphtha

Sometimes called "alkyd varnish" after the resin in it, oil varnish is a good middle-of-the-road finish that is pretty durable, fairly easy to use, and moderately flexible. It is designed to be brushed on, but you can also wipe it on and off like a Danish oil, though it builds up faster and

Oil varnish and wiping varnish

Polyurethane gel

dries slower. Varnish is usually amber in color and, like oils, brings out the depth in wood. It is a good choice for moderate-use furniture, such as in living rooms, dining rooms, and bedrooms, where depth and sheen are important.

Polyurethane Gel

Durability: moderate water, scratch, solvent, heat, and stain resistance

Apply with: rag

Solvent: none needed; cleanup with mineral spirits or naphtha

The gel version of polyurethane varnish eliminates the solvent smell and the "plastic" appearance of polyurethane. Because it is wiped on and tends to be applied thinly, it also loses much of liquid polyurethane's durability. Polyurethane

gel is probably the easiest finish to apply and looks about the same as Danish oil on wood. Each coat takes several hours to dry, but the thick consistency and thin application prevent dust from settling into the film while it is curing. It is a good choice for fairly low-wear surfaces, like boxes, chairs, and shelving, where a natural woody look is favored.

Polyurethane Varnish

Durability: very good water, scratch, solvent, and heat resistance, good stain resistance

Apply with: rag or brush

Solvent: mineral spirits, naphtha

Polyurethane varnish is the most popular brushed finish on the market today. Slightly gray/amber, it is a bit more plastic-

Polyurethane varnish

I made a wall ornament for my wife and finished it with interior polyurethane varnish. Now she wants to hang it outside on the covered porch. Do I need to refinish it with exterior varnish?

No, not as long as it is out of direct sunlight. Interior oil polyurethane is flexible enough to tolerate the wood movement outdoors. However, it is not designed to withstand strong, direct sunlight. Exterior varnish is made with aliphatic resin, which resists UV degrade, while interior is often made from aromatic resins, which break down in direct sunlight. Since the porch is covered, the ornament will not be in direct sunlight and the interior polyurethane will be fine. Conversely, you can always use exterior varnish indoors. The only drawback is that is usually more expensive.

looking than oil varnish, shellac, or lacquer, but it shares oil's ability to perk up wood. Polyurethane's exceptional durability makes it the best brushable option for high-wear surfaces, like bar tops, dining tables, and kitchen cabinets. Though it can be applied with a rag, it is most often brushed on. Each coat should be allowed to dry overnight.

Shellac

Durability: good water, scratch, and stain resistance, fair solvent resistance, poor heat resistance

Apply with: rag, brush, spray gun, or "French polish" pad

Solvent: alcohol

Shellac comes both premixed and in flakes that you mix with alcohol and is available in a range of colors from garnet to very light amber. It is a beautiful, clear finish that does much to bring out the best in wood and looks good both thin and woody, like an oil finish, or thick and glossy. Shellac is easy to apply by wiping, brushing, or spraying, or on a pad as a traditional French polish, and it dries very fast. Its sealing properties are legendary—it will seal in stains, oil, wax, and a variety of contaminants. For that reason, shellac is widely used as a sealer under other finishes. It has low heat resistance and will dissolve in alcohol and strong alkaline solutions, so it's not good for many high-wear surfaces.

Freshly mixed shellac with the natural wax removed has very good resistance to acids and water spotting, but as the liquid

Is Shellac Really Made of Bug Doots?

Well,…no. But it is made by insects. And it is a fascinating process.

A small bug called *Laccifer lacca*, about the size of an apple seed, swarms on certain trees in India and Thailand. It secretes a hard translucent covering that protects it during its larval stage. Once the bug matures, it breaks out and flies away, leaving the covering behind. The natives collect the branches and scrape off the crusty reddish material.

The scrapings, which contain bits of bark and the odd bug leg, along with shellac resin, are called "seedlac." Seedlac is melted and strained to make shellac. Along with the shellac resin there is a naturally occurring wax and a deep red dye. For many years the dye was more valuable than the resin, but the invention of aniline dyes in the mid 1800s changed that.

The strained material is dried in sheets, broken up into flakes, and graded for color and purity.

Some is further refined to remove the wax to make dewaxed shellac. Or the natural dye can be filtered out to create blonde or super blonde shellac, and the material can even be bleached to make "white" shellac.

Once all this is done, we take the flakes, dissolve them in alcohol, and voila!—shellac. Once dry, shellac is completely nontoxic. In fact, more of it is used to coat candy (as confectioner's glaze) and time-release medicines than is used on furniture.

The instructions that came with the shellac flakes I bought say to dissolve them in alcohol. Do I need to buy anhydrous alcohol, or can I use rubbing alcohol?

The best, cheapest option for dissolving shellac flakes or thinning premixed shellac is denatured alcohol. Rubbing alcohol won't work and anhydrous is overkill.

Denatured alcohol is primarily ethanol, the same alcohol we drink in wine, beer, and harder stuff. To avoid the liquor consumption tax, denatured alcohol has 1% or 2% poison added to it to make it undrinkable. It is an ideal solvent for whenever you need alcohol.

Anhydrous, or water-free alcohol, is much more expensive, and though it will work, it is not necessary. Shellac will tolerate as much as 10% water in its alcohol and still work just fine. Standard denatured alcohol rarely has more than 5% water, and usually only 3%. At the far end of the acceptable spectrum is Everclear, sold in liquor stores as a mixer, which is 90% alcohol and 10% water.

Rubbing alcohol, on the other hand, is 50% alcohol and 50% water. Leave that in the medicine chest. It has too much water for shellac.

ages in the can, the water resistance diminishes. It is a good finish for "show" pieces where appearance is important, and for moderate-wear items like occasional tables or boxes that will not be subjected to harsh chemicals or alcohol. Because it is completely nontoxic—and even edible—it is an ideal finish for children's toys, cribs, cradles, and food-contact items.

Spar Varnish

Durability: very good water, solvent, heat, and stain resistance, fair scratch resistance

Apply with: brush

Solvent: mineral spirits or naphtha

Shellac

Spar varnish

The traditional varnish for spars and brightwork on boats, spar varnish is the softest and most flexible of the varnishes. Though it does not have good scratch resistance, its flexibility enables it to tolerate lots of wood movement. The ingredients of traditional spar varnish, tung oil and phenolic resin, have a natural tolerance for ultraviolet light, so the finish holds up well outdoors without peeling or cracking. Like all oil-based varnishes, spar varnish dries slowly and brings out depth in wood while adding a slightly reddish amber color. Spar varnish is an ideal finish for outdoor furniture, such as patio benches and Adirondack chairs, and for exterior doors and ornaments.

Coping with Sunlight

The thing that sets exterior finishes apart from interior finishes is their ability to resist the aging effects of sunlight. The ultraviolet (UV) rays of the sun fade colors, yellow clear coatings, make some finishes and woods go dark, and cause finishes to crack, peel, and turn chalky.

Some finishes, like spar varnish, have a natural resistance to UV destruction. That means the finish will not break down easily in sunlight, but it does *not* mean that it will protect the wood or stain from fading. To do that, you must use a finish that has UV blockers or absorbers in it. Many, but not all, exterior finishes contain UV blockers and say so on the label. These will help delay UV damage but will not stop it entirely or forever.

Similarly, most pigmented stains will not fade in sunlight. However, almost all dyes will fade, some faster than others. Choose pigmented stains for exterior work or for pieces sitting in strong, direct sunlight, even indoors.

Waterborne lacquer

We did a white pickled finish on our oak hall stand. What sort of clear coat will protect it without changing the color or yellowing later?

Waterborne lacquers and polyurethanes, CAB lacquer, and acrylic lacquers are all virtually clear and will stay that way. Avoid nitrocellulose lacquer, or any oil-based finish, such as oil varnish or polyurethane.

Waterborne Lacquer

Durability: good water, scratch, and stain resistance, moderate solvent and heat resistance

Apply with: paint pad, sponge, nylon brush, or spray gun

Solvent: none required, but most will tolerate small amounts of water, glycol ethers, propylene glycol, and lacquer thinner

Nonflammable, low-odor waterborne lacquers are an attempt to make lacquer less dangerous and less offensive both to us and to the environment. You can think of them as a clear version of latex paint. Waterborne lacquer does not flow out as easily or as well as lacquer and does not add the depth to wood that shellac, lacquer, and oils impart. Although it looks milky white in the can, it dries almost water clear. While this looks good on very light and white woods, darker woods like walnut and rosewood appear pale and wan under most waterborne lacquer. Waterborne lacquer dries about as fast as lacquer but should be sanded between coats. It has about the same wear properties as lacquer and works well for moderate-wear furniture that you'd find in the bedroom, living room, office, or den.

Waterborne Polyurethane

Durability: very good scratch and heat resistance, good water and solvent resistance, moderate stain resistance

Apply with: paint pad, sponge, nylon brush, or spray gun

Solvent: none required, but most will tolerate small amounts of water and propylene glycol

This nonflammable, low-odor alternative to polyurethane lacks the oil-based version's depth and richness but retains most of its durability. Waterborne polyurethane is clear with a slight bluish cast that makes it look good on light and white woods but pale and wan on dark woods, such as walnut and rosewood. Like waterborne lacquer, it is usually milky white in the can, dries dust free in about 10 minutes, and must be sanded between coats. It is a good substitute for oil polyurethane and will tolerate the abuse typical of kitchens and dining-room tables.

Waterborne Polyurethane/Lacquer with Crosslinker

Durability: excellent stain, heat, scratch, water, and solvent resistance

Apply with: paint pad, sponge, nylon brush, or spray gun

Solvent: none required

Adding a crosslinker to waterborne lacquer or polyurethane makes it the low-odor, nonflammable equivalent of conversion varnish. Originally sold as hardwood floor finish, it has crossed over into the furniture field. You must add a crosslinker to the mix before applying it, but it dries fast and clear with a slight bluish cast. Like all waterbornes, it may look somewhat pale on dark woods. It is durable enough for very high-wear surfaces, like bar tops, kitchen counters, commercial furniture, and floors.

Wax

Durability: poor stain, heat, scratch, water, and solvent resistance

Apply with: rag

Solvent: mineral spirits or naphtha

Wax is a very weak but very easy to apply finish. It is most often used as a sacrificial "scratch deflector" over other

The left half of this cherry board was finished with an oil-based finish and the right half with a waterborne finish. The difference is strikingly apparent.

Waterborne polyurethane

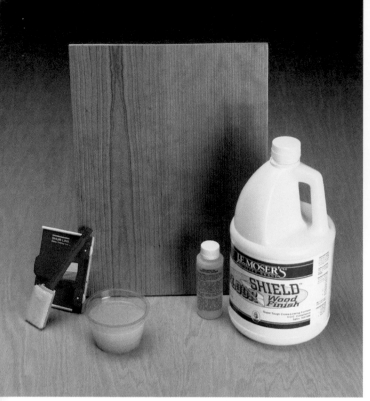

Waterborne polyurethane/lacquer with crosslinker   **Wax**

I have some old, partially used finish cans on the shelf. How long can I store them before they are no good anymore?

Shelf life varies among finishes and brands. Here's a list of some average storage times of common materials, starting with the shortest shelf life. You might be able to get away with using older materials, but if you want to play it safe, follow these general guidelines.

- Shellac: 6 to 9 months
- Waterborne coatings: 18 months to 2 years
- Lacquer: 2 to 3 years
- Oil varnish, polyurethane, linseed oil, and Danish oil: 3 to 5 years
- Paste wax: indefinite, as long as it hasn't hardened in the can

finishes but offers little or no protection on its own. Paste wax comes in a variety of colors from almost clear to dark brown. The clearer versions leave wood looking almost completely natural, without the "wet" appearance of oils, lacquers, and varnishes, and with little or no gloss. Choose wax for very low-wear items where the natural wood look is prized, such as art turnings, "treen," and exposed ceiling beams. It is also good as a protective lubricant over more durable finishes, like shellac, lacquer, and varnish.

The chart on the facing page will help you choose the best finish for each of your woodworking projects. Take it with you when you head to the store.

Choosing a Finish

	Evaporative or reactive	Thin with	Durability	Stain resistance	Heat resistance	Flammable
Catalyzed lacquer/ conversion varnish/ precatalyzed lacquer	R	MEK, special lacquer thinner	excellent	excellent	excellent	yes
Danish oil	R	mineral spirits, naphtha	poor	poor	moderate	yes
Lacquer	E	lacquer thinner	very good	very good	poor	yes
Oils (linseed, tung, walnut)	R	mineral spirits, naphtha	poor	poor	moderate	no
Oil varnish and wiping varnish	R	mineral spirits, naphtha	good	good	good	yes
Polyurethane gel	R	none	moderate	moderate	moderate	no
Polyurethane varnish	R	mineral spirits, naphtha	very good	good	very good	yes
Shellac	E	alcohol	good	good	poor	yes
Spar varnish	R	mineral spirits, naphtha	good	very good	very good	yes
Waterborne lacquer	E	none	good	good	moderate	no
Waterborne polyurethane	E	none	very good	moderate	very good	no
Waterborne polyurethane/ lacquer with crosslinker	R	none	excellent	excellent	excellent	no
Wax	E	mineral spirits, naphtha	poor	poor	poor	no

Tools of the Trade

Anything that you use while getting finish from the can to the wood is a finishing tool. Some tools are obvious. It will be no surprise to anyone to see brushes and spray guns among the entries in this chapter. But there are other "tools," like masking tape and goggles, that are every bit as important.

Finishing puts you in contact with chemicals that are not particularly friendly to humans. Try as we might, we can't change that entirely. Using good safety equipment, like goggles, gloves, and respirators, puts a barrier between you and what can harm you. The right gear can make the difference between an activity that is hazardous and one that is pleasant.

Once we've protected ourselves, we can get down to the business of getting finish onto the wood. Our application tools can be anything from a simple rag or paper towel to sophisticated specialty brushes and spray guns. Some finishes do better with a particular application method, and some tools lend themselves to certain working environments. Choosing the right tool for the job can make a world of difference in the results you get and how long it takes to get them. And then there are the "helpers." Things like masking tape and strainers don't apply finish, but they help make the process go more smoothly—in more ways than one.

Safety Equipment

Whenever there's a chance that a chemical can splash into your eyes, wear goggles. That includes when you are mixing, stirring, pouring, or adding solvent to a finish, as well as whenever you use paint removers.

Eye protection and gloves should be used whenever there is a chance that a chemical can splash into your eyes or onto your hands.

If you are putting your hands in chemicals, put them in gloves first. Some solvents, like alcohol and methylene chloride, can enter your body by going through your skin. Others, like lacquer thinner, will dry or chap your skin and may cause rashes. Use tough neoprene gloves for paint remover or harsh solvents and vinyl or latex gloves for milder solvents, like alcohol and lacquer thinner. I keep a box of inexpensive throwaway vinyl gloves for staining, too. Even if the stain is harmless, like some waterborne stains, the gloves keep my hands clean.

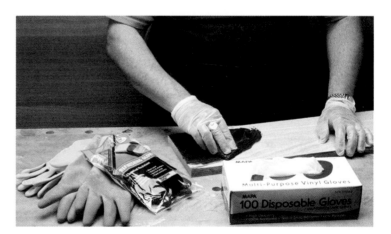

Inexpensive throwaway vinyl gloves are great for staining, but use tough neoprene gloves for paint remover or harsh solvents and vinyl or latex gloves for milder solvents, like alcohol and lacquer thinner.

Some respirators incorporate a face mask as well, eliminating the need for goggles. The standard organic respirator in the center is flanked by a face shield/respirator on the right and a full hood with separate air supply on the left.

Many of the solvents we use can cause long-term health problems with too much exposure. Solvent evaporates from finish whether you spray, brush, or wipe it on, but an organic vapor cartridge mask will block most of these vapors. Bear in mind that the useful life of the cartridge is based on exposure to the air, whether or not you are wearing it. When you take the mask off, seal it in a plastic bag. Most cartridges last for about eight hours of use. If you can smell the solvent while wearing the mask, it is time to replace the cartridge.

Application Tools

The first chapter in this book gave you enough information to make an enlightened choice about what finish you want to use. This chapter will help you decide what to use for putting your chosen finish onto the wood. Depending on the surface you are coating and what you coat it with, you may want to use a simple rag or piece of steel wool, a brush, or a spray gun. Those last two aren't so simple. There are many types of brushes and almost as many configurations of spray guns, but with enough information you can make wise choices when it comes to applying finishes.

Cloth Rags and Paper Towels

There are times when the simplest applicator is best. Cloth rags and paper towels are great for putting on (and wiping off) stain and many types of finish, including shellac, varnish, gel coatings, oil, and wax. In fact, I almost always apply my first coat of shellac by rag, no matter what method I use for the final coats.

My favorite rags for staining and finishing are tight-weave cotton cheesecloth (see the photo on the facing page). They easily absorb a lot of stain or finish and leave a minimum of lint. I use the same cloth, formed into a ball and covered with a layer of linen, to make a French polish pad (see pp. 126-127 for more on French polishing).

There are always a few rolls of heavy-duty paper towels in my shop as well. They are particularly handy for wiping off excess stain, oil, and even paint-remover residue. And paper towels are cheap enough that you have no qualms about grabbing a fresh one when you need a clean wiper for absorbing and removing material.

One word of warning: Rags or paper towels with oil on them are subject to spontaneous combustion. Either incinerate them immediately or hang them out to dry, one layer thick. Once they are dry, you can put them out with the trash.

Sandpaper, Steel Wool, and Nylon Abrasive Pads

There are times when you can kill two birds with one stone. Applying wax, stain, or finish with an abrasive material is one such time. You get the finish on the wood and smooth out the surface all at once.

Sanding boiled linseed oil into wood is an old finisher's trick commonly used for oiled walnut, but it works on almost any wood. Wipe on a coat of oil and, instead of wiping it off, sand it with 400-grit wet/dry sandpaper. It creates a slurry of sanding dust mixed with oil that fills the pores more quickly and leaves the wood smooth. Of course, sandpaper is also used to smooth wood before finishing, but that's covered in the section on preparing the wood (see pp. 66-75).

You can use 0000 steel wool to rub a finish to satin and apply paste wax in one step. That's described in detail in the chapter on rubbing out the finish (see pp. 167-170). Fine nylon abrasive pads are great for applying certain types of stains onto raw wood, especially gels and water-borne stains. The pad reduces raised grain and stays wet far longer than a rag or paper towel. Rags and paper towels tend to wick off water and solvent, and before long the stain is thicker than it should be. Nylon pads hold the water and solvent and allow you to stain larger areas more evenly.

Paint pads come in a variety of shapes and sizes. They apply a lot of material very quickly and work very well with clear waterborne coatings.

Is there anything wrong with using those gray, foam-on-a-stick brushes? They are so much cheaper than real brushes, and you don't have to clean them.

If you like them and they work for you, that's what matters. I find foam brushes helpful for "cheap brush" applications, but not for fine brush work. For instance, foam brushes are great for applying stain and bleach and for laying down the first coat of varnish, Danish oil, and even waterbornes. First coats don't matter quite as much, since they mostly absorb into the wood and will probably be sanded later. I find foam brushes don't work as well for final coats, nor for anything other than flat surfaces. (They will not get into carvings or flutes the way a bristle brush will.) Foam cannot be used with lacquer because it melts in lacquer thinner.

Paint Pads and Foam Brushes

As waterborne finishes have become more popular, so have paint pads. Paint pads apply a lot of material very quickly and work very well with clear waterborne coatings. Perhaps that is because they were developed for latex paint, another waterborne finish. The pads do not drip as easily as a brush and cause less foaming, a common problem with waterbornes. Although you may be tempted to manipulate a brush back and forth, the best technique with a paint pad is to lay the finish down on the first stroke, and then repeat the stroke once more in the same direction to smooth it out.

Foam brushes look like a brush-shaped chunk of dark gray foam rubber on a wooden stick. Though foam brushes are

FINISHING TALES

Drew's Revenge

My boss and I were out on an installation that day, so we didn't know that Roger had called in "sick." We knew why, though. The day before, he had failed miserably at getting our new waterborne lacquer to spray evenly onto a series of huge doors designed to hold glass panels. The doors took two people to move in and out of the spray booth, and no matter what Roger did, they came out looking like orange peel. I guess we were all sick of that job.

We realized that meant that Drew, a new employee in the finishing shop, was left alone to re-coat those monsters. We figured there was no way he could do it, so at break time, we called Kaitlin, the office manager, to see how he was faring. We expected the worst.

"Drew says he'll be finished with the frames today," Kaitlin

happily informed us. "He asked for $10 early this morning, made a trip to the hardware store, and has been at work ever since. I looked at the frames a few minutes ago, and they look great."

We were dumbstruck. What sort of $10 hardware store miracle could enable a man to haul around huge wet door frames alone? Besides, we figured, how could a new guy have any better luck spraying than Roger?

Drew was just cleaning up when we arrived back at the shop. The frames were exactly where we had left them the day before, spread out on sawhorses. Each had two new coats of waterborne lacquer, and the finish was smooth and even. Drew had coated them all alone, used half the amount of lacquer we expected to need, and there wasn't a hint of overspray in the air.

"How did you do it?" we asked in amazement. Drew held up a cheap, $5 paint pad with a white nylon nap on a bright red plastic holder. Rather than move the frames to the finish, he had brought the finish to the frames.

"Paint pads work great with this waterborne stuff," Drew pointed out. "After all, isn't that what latex paint is? Besides," he went on, "the pad costs only five bucks, so you can throw it out if you don't feel like cleaning the thing."

Drew had his coat on and was halfway out the door before my boss shook off his stupor enough to call after him. "What was the other $5 for?" he asked.

Drew shrugged slightly as he calmly turned to answer. "Coffee and doughnuts. I woke up late and didn't have time for breakfast."

not as versatile as a good bristle brush, many finishers find they work well with stains, gels, and oil-based varnishes. Stay away from lacquer, though, because the solvents in it may dissolve the brush. One of the strong arguments for foam brushes is that their low price makes it cost-effective to throw them out rather than clean them.

Brushes

Whoever first took a fistful of animal fur and attached it to a stick to make a brush did us all a favor. Brushes are wonderful finishing tools. They transfer virtually any finish to virtually any shape surface and lay it out smoothly without wasting any of it.

Yesterday in the hardware store I stood before a wall full of brushes that ranged from $2 to $17—all for the same size brush. I understand that there are differences, but how much does it matter? Are there certain jobs where it is okay to use a cheap brush? Which things really demand a high-quality brush?

Good brushes show their mettle when you apply topcoats, but throwaway brushes are fine for hard-to-clean uses like staining.

A well-made, well-shaped brush makes a world of difference when you are trying to lay down a smooth coat of varnish. It holds more material, feeds the material out more evenly, and leaves fewer brush marks. I use only the best brushes for applying topcoats, whether they are of varnish, polyurethane, shellac, lacquer, or waterbornes. By cleaning the brushes and caring for them properly, they last for years and end up being cheaper in the long run. I have several brushes that are more than 15 years old and still in great shape.

But cheap throwaway brushes have their place as well. If you are using a material that will not clean up well and where the final application is not an issue, throwaways are fine. For example, you can use a cheap brush to apply stain or pore filler, since it will be wiped off later anyway.

Anatomy of a Brush

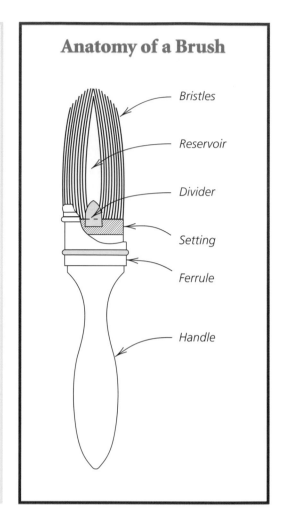

- Bristles
- Reservoir
- Divider
- Setting
- Ferrule
- Handle

Brushes come in many shapes and sizes and are made of a variety of bristle materials to handle various tasks. Which size or shape you choose and how you use it is purely a matter of personal style. If it fits comfortably in your hand and works for you, it is right. The information in this section is to help you make some good choices, enjoy using what you've chosen, and care for the brushes so they'll last a long time.

Buying a brush The shape and type of bristle you choose should relate to its use. Generally, brushes with flat or cut bundles of bristles are best for thick paints or where you want brush marks to show. Chisel-end bundles make it easier to flow out thin finishes, like lacquer, shellac, and varnish, without brush marks.

There are three common bristle shapes. Tipped bristles are chopped off like those on a toothbrush. They are best for thick paints where brush marks won't show or

This gallery of brushes contains some of the many styles and configurations that the author uses for various finishing tasks.

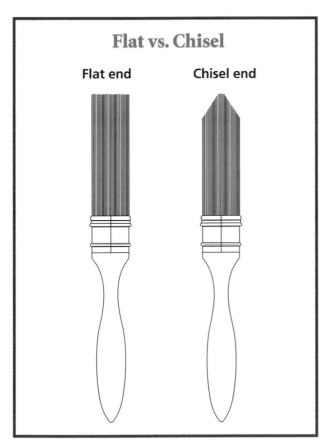

Flat vs. Chisel

Flat end

Chisel end

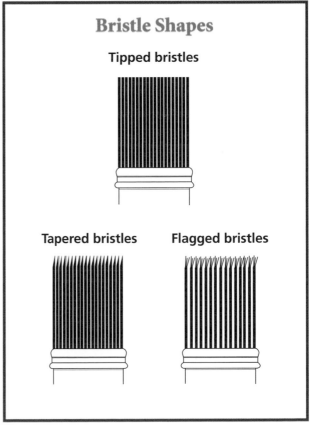

Bristle Shapes

Tipped bristles

Tapered bristles

Flagged bristles

don't matter. Tapered bristles come to a point at the end. They are good for smooth finish application and best for waterborne finishes. Flagged bristles look like hair with "split ends." They leave the smoothest surface with the fewest brush marks and are favored for varnish, shellac, and lacquer work. However, flagged ends tend to cause foaming in waterborne coatings by creating tiny air bubbles that stay in the film.

Look for long bristles that are smooth, springy, and hold their shape. Longer bristles hold more material and allow the finish to flow better than short bristles. Of course, not all types of hair grow the same length, so length is relative. Cheap brushes often sport bristles that are too short to work well.

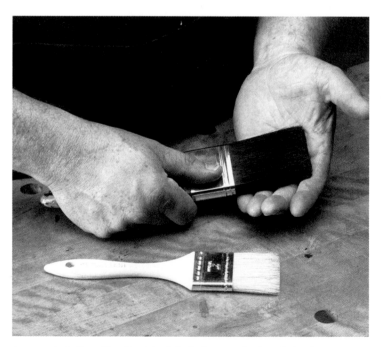

Longer bristles, like the black bristles on the brush in the author's hand, hold more material and allow the finish to flow better than the short bristles in the brush on the bench.

On a chisel end, the hair should be set in tiers so that the ends of the bristles form the shape. The hair should not be cut to a chisel shape. And tugging lightly on the bristles should not dislodge any. If it is a natural bristle brush, the hair should feel silky, as if it had just walked off the set of a shampoo and conditioner commercial on television. Better brushes often have the type of bristle marked on the handle.

Most finishers, myself included, prefer natural bristle brushes for all solvent-based finishes. A wide variety of animal hair is used for natural bristle brushes, but the following are some of the more common ones.

China bristle is hog hair and comes in white, gray, and black (the color doesn't make any difference). China is a good, springy, medium-soft bristle and is the most common natural hair used in lacquer and varnish brushes. Look for hair that is at least 2½ in. (65mm) long. *Fitch* is another name for polecat or skunk. The bristles are usually shorter (1¾ in./45mm) and are thin, soft, and pliable. I like fitch for applying shellac. *Badger* is distinctively two-toned and stiffer and springier than China. Typical lengths run around 2 in. (50mm). Badger is popular for oil varnish. *Camel hair*, which does not come from a camel, is a very soft hair good for smaller application and touch-up brushes. History tells us the brush was invented by a man named Kamel, and over time the spelling was altered. The original Kamel brushes were squirrel hair, but these days most are pony hair. **Sable**, a weasel-like relative of the marten, is unusually resilient and can be shaped to a fine, sharp point. A good red sable touch-up brush will allow you to lay down an extremely thin grain line with its well-defined point. **Squirrel hair** is used for some specialty brushes, like dagger stripers and quills, both of which are used for pinstriping.

Natural bristles are animal hair, and, like our own hair, they tend to splay in water. For that reason, we generally use synthetic bristle brushes for waterborne coatings. Synthetic bristles are usually either nylon, polyester, or a nylon-polyester mix. They can be used with any coating but are almost a must with finishes that contain water. Nylon is softer, and I prefer it for clear waterborne coatings. Polyester is stiffer and springier and works better with thicker coatings. The nylon-poly blends fall somewhere in between.

Caring for your brushes A good brush, like a fine chisel or plane, is an investment in a tool that can give you many years of satisfying service. If you follow the proper care procedure, your brushes will last a long time and always handle the way they did when they were new.

Before you use the brush—the first time and every time—soak the bristles up to the ferrule in whatever solvent is used to thin or clean up the coating. This is

On the bench, clockwise from right: black long China bristle, white shorter China bristle, fitch, badger, and camel. In the box, from bottom to top: sable touch-up brush, dagger striper, quill.

Natural bristles, like the brush on the left, tend to splay when water gets on them.

Before dipping the brush into the finish, soak the bristles up to the ferrule in the appropriate solvent, then squeeze out the excess solvent. Keep a can of solvent handy for rejuvenating the brush while you work.

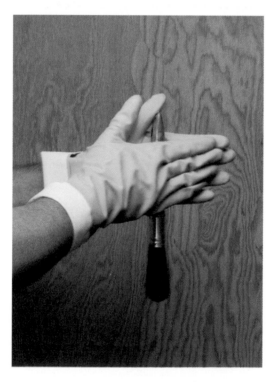

To remove the solvent, spin the brush until the bristles look and feel clean but damp.

true for both natural bristles and synthetic bristles. Soak in lacquer thinner for lacquer, alcohol for shellac, mineral spirits for oil varnish, and water for waterborne coatings. Squeeze out any excess liquid, but don't spin the brush dry.

This presoaking loads the reservoir and wets the bristles. The solvent in the reservoir will help flow the finish off the ends of the bristles and will prevent the upper edge of the finish from forming a hard, dry crust near the ferrule. It will make the brush perform better and make it much easier to clean once you are done.

During the time you are using the brush, dip only one-third of the length of the bristles into the coating. After working with the brush for about 10 or 15 minutes, you'll notice the finish starting to creep up toward the ferrule; eventually, it will dry and form a crust on the "inactive" section of the bristles. When you notice this happening, stop and quickly clean the brush by scraping the finish back into the container and then massaging the bristles in the clean-up solvent. Squeeze out the excess as before and reload the brush with finish. It takes less than 30 seconds to rejuvenate the brush, but you are guaranteed an easy cleanup and get the feeling you are always working with a fresh brush. In other words, it takes less time than it does to stop and resharpen your chisel in the middle of a long session of cutting wood.

After you finish, remove all the excess coating you can by scraping the brush

Wrapping a Brush

1 After spinning out the water, wrap the brush in absorbent brown paper.

2 Locate the tips of the bristles and fold the paper over on itself about 1 in. past them.

3 Secure the wrap with some tape or a rubber band around the ferrule.

across the edge of the container and brush out what you can onto cardboard, scrap wood, or newspaper. Now get the brush as clean as you can by massaging the bristles in the appropriate solvent. Shake and spin the brush to remove the solvent until the bristles look and feel clean but damp.

Immediately wash the entire length of the bristles in warm soapy water. I like to use soap designed for hair, like shaving soap or shampoo. Rinse and repeat until the soap sudses easily. Now rinse out the soap and shake off and spin out the water.

While the brush is still damp, wrap it in absorbent paper (brown paper bags are perfect). Wrap the paper around the brush extending from the middle of the ferrule well past the ends of the bristles (see the photos above). Feel for the end of the bristles and fold the paper over about 1 in. past them. Some tape, a rubber band, or just the weight of the brush will hold the paper in place until the brush is dry. The paper will allow the water to escape while "setting" the bristles back to their original shape. When you go to use it next, the brush will be just like new— clean, supple, and correctly shaped.

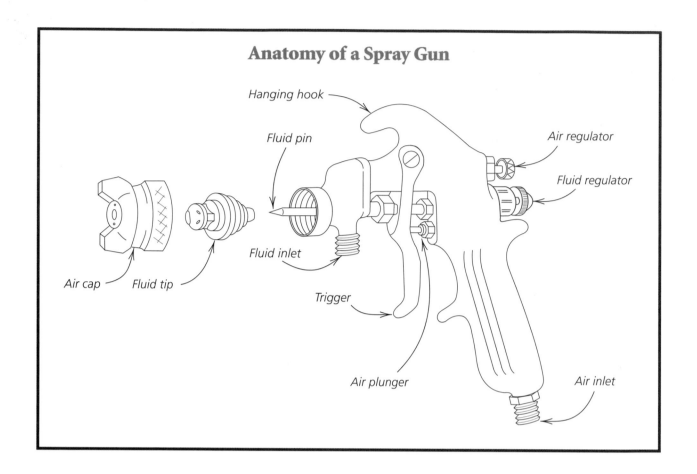

Anatomy of a Spray Gun

Hanging hook

Fluid pin

Air regulator

Fluid regulator

Air cap

Fluid tip

Fluid inlet

Trigger

Air plunger

Air inlet

Spray Guns

A spray gun atomizes liquid finish into tiny droplets and directs them in a controlled pattern toward the wood. By spraying, you can: coat more area faster and uniformly; use fast-drying finishes formulated specifically for spraying; and apply a satin finish with no brush or steel-wool marks.

The price for these advantages is higher energy consumption, contaminated air, and wasted material. Spray guns require energy to power them and a spray booth and fan to evacuate solvents and over-spray that misses the wood. When you use

a brush, virtually all of the finish you buy ends up on the wood. When you use a spray gun, from one-third to three-quarters of the finish ends up either outside via the fan or settled on the spray-booth walls and floor. That does not mean you shouldn't spray finish. It only means you should know the cost up front.

How spray guns work When you pull the trigger of a spray gun, it draws back a fluid pin and pushes in an air plunger. As a result, a stream of air and a stream of finish are both directed to the front of the gun (as shown in the drawing on the facing page). There, the fluid tip and the air

How a Spray Gun Works

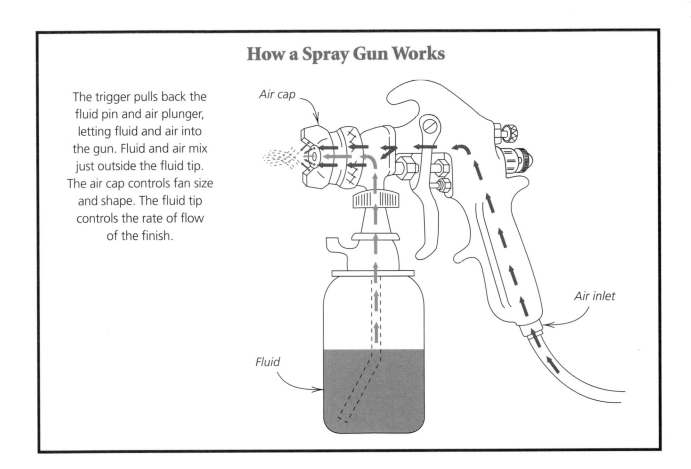

The trigger pulls back the fluid pin and air plunger, letting fluid and air into the gun. Fluid and air mix just outside the fluid tip. The air cap controls fan size and shape. The fluid tip controls the rate of flow of the finish.

Air cap

Air inlet

Fluid

cap work together to create a pattern of atomized finish. Fluid is fed to the tip in one of three ways: siphon, gravity, or pressure (see the drawing on p. 34).

Siphon-feed guns have a cup of finish suspended below the gun. As the gun directs a stream of concentrated air across the tip of a tube going into the finish, it creates a partial vacuum, which draws the finish up the tube and into the fluid tip. Since creating the vacuum uses up air, siphon-feed guns require more air than the other two types. Siphon-feed guns won't work upside down (see the drawing on p. 35).

Gravity-feed guns have a cup suspended above the gun. Gravity causes the finish to flow down into the fluid tip. All of the air from a gravity-feed gun goes into atomizing the liquid, not transporting it. One company, DeVilbiss, offers a sealed liner that even enables its gravity-feed gun to spray upside down.

Pressure-feed guns use a pressurized cup or pot. The air pressure in this container forces the finish through a tube and up to the fluid tip. The container can be attached to the gun or attached separately via a fluid hose. Pressure-feed guns with separate pots allow you to spray with the gun upside down.

Gravity-, Siphon-, and Pressure-Feed Guns

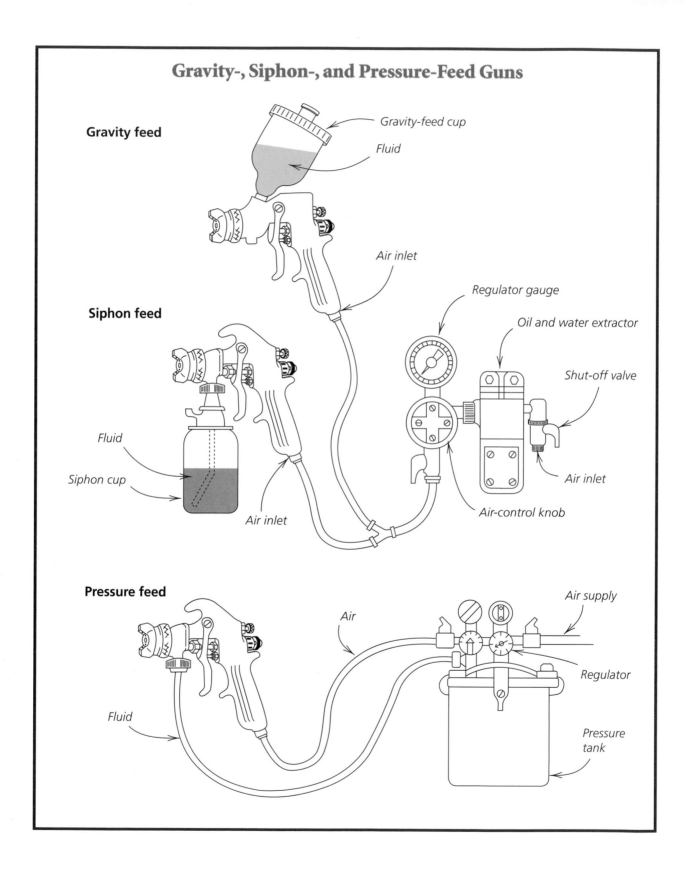

Gravity feed

Gravity-feed cup

Fluid

Air inlet

Siphon feed

Regulator gauge

Oil and water extractor

Shut-off valve

Fluid

Siphon cup

Air inlet

Air-control knob

Air inlet

Pressure feed

Air

Air supply

Regulator

Fluid

Pressure tank

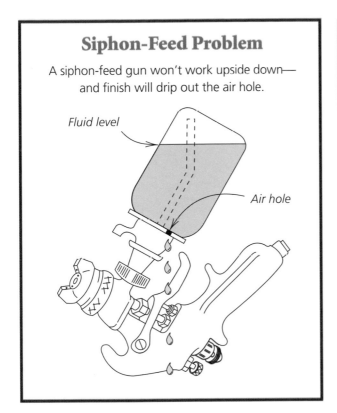

Siphon-Feed Problem

A siphon-feed gun won't work upside down—and finish will drip out the air hole.

Fluid level

Air hole

I've been thinking about switching from the lacquer I currently spray to a waterborne coating. A friend told me that I need to have an HVLP gun in order to spray waterborne coatings. What type should I buy?

You do NOT need an HVLP gun to spray waterborne coatings. HVLP guns are more efficient and save material, so they may well be a good investment over the long run. But it is not true that you must have one for spraying waterbornes. Your standard gun will do just fine, provided the fluid pathways are stainless steel—regular steel can rust. I would suggest buying a smaller (1mm) stainless-steel fluid tip for the gun. I'd also plan to spend some time spraying scrap wood to learn the differences between the ways solvent-borne and water-borne finishes flow out.

Standard vs. HVLP guns Standard or high-pressure spray guns, which have been in use since the 1920s, are quite versatile. They can spray both thick and thin finishes merely by adjusting the pressure to the gun. Their downside is that they are wasteful. Standard spray guns force finish out the tip at pressures that range from 25 psi to 80 psi (pounds per square inch). Although some of the finish lands on the wood, much of it either misses or, due to the high pressure, bounces back off the surface. Typically, only about 25% of the finish ends up on the wood. Seventy-five percent waste is a high price to pay for speed.

HVLP (high-volume, low-pressure) guns spray more efficiently. By reducing the amount of pressure and replacing it with a higher volume of air, they can deposit about 65% of the finish on the wood. As a result, switching to an HVLP gun is likely to cut your finish usage in half. Furthermore, it will substantially reduce the amount of overspray that will fill the air in your shop or spray booth. A good conversion-type HVLP gun (see p. 36) will spray any material that a standard gun can spray and do it far more efficiently.

HVLP guns get their air in one of two ways: via a turbine or by converting compressed air to low-pressure air. *Turbine-driven guns* are attached via a large-diameter (1-in.) hose to what is essentially the exhaust port of a vacuum cleaner-type motor. The motor generates a large volume of air (65 cubic feet per

I purchased an HVLP spray gun with a 1.4mm needle and cap and was told this was good for waterborne finishes. It seems to work okay, but I get a lot of orange peel. What should I do?

You will probably get better atomization with a 1.0mm fluid tip. I prefer a 1.0mm fluid opening for waterborne and 1.4mm or 1.5mm for lacquer. The smaller fluid tip results in better atomization and less orange peel. The other options are to turn up the air pressure, if you can, and thin out the material, either of which should reduce orange peel.

minute, or cfm) at fairly low pressure (3 psi to 10 psi). Turbines are sold by motor size and number of "stages." The motor size determines the volume of air produced, while the number of stages affects the pressure. A two-stage turbine will produce 4 psi or 5 psi, while a three-stage may produce 6 psi or 7 psi. Higher pressure at the tip usually means better atomization, and thick finishes often require higher tip pressures.

Turbine-driven HVLP guns are portable but have limited versatility. The turbine is usually fairly small and light and will plug into any 110-volt outlet. However, the number of stages on the turbine limits what viscosity (thickness) of material can be sprayed. If the turbine produces only 5 psi, it will spray only fairly thin finishes smoothly.

Conversion guns are attached by a standard ¼-in. or ⅜-in. hose to an air compressor. They convert high-pressure air (60 psi to 80 psi) so that the pressure exiting the tip of the gun is only about

10 psi. These guns use from 7 cfm to 20 cfm, a larger volume of air than standard guns use. While a standard spray gun can work with a small 1-hp (horsepower) compressor, many HVLP guns need a larger (3-hp to 5-hp) compressor to work properly. By changing the pressure going into the gun, you can change the pressure exiting the tip. A conversion gun can put out a full 10 psi at the tip, which means it can spray the same wide range of thick and thin finishes that a standard high-pressure gun can handle.

Conversion HVLP guns are versatile but not very portable. They will spray almost any viscosity of material well. However, they must be connected to a compressor, which is usually far less portable than a turbine. Furthermore, due to the inefficiency of the conversion, the gun may use a fairly large volume of air, which means it needs a relatively large (3-hp to 5-hp) compressor.

Buying a spray gun The main thing to consider when you buy a gun is what you will want to spray with it. The fluid tip on a gun controls how much liquid passes through it, while the air cap controls the shape of the exiting air. These two elements work together, and by changing them you can vary what finishes you are able to spray as well as the spray pattern itself.

If you are likely to spray finishes with different viscosities, or if you want to alter the size of the spray pattern, look for a gun that offers several air-cap and fluid-

Sample Air-Cap Selection Guide

| Typical materials | Viscosity[1] | | | Air-cap model no. | Air-cap part no. | Operating range | | Typical pattern size in. (mm) | Fluid-tip no. & size in. (mm) | Type of feed |
	Low	Med	High			PSI	SCFM			
Adhesives		•	•	24	AV-40-24	50	14	4-7 (100-175)	D .086 (2.2) E .070 (1.8) FF .055 (1.4)	Pressure
Enamels, lacquers, metallics	•	•		30	MB-4039-30	50	12	8-10 (200-250)	EX .070 (1.8) FF .055 (1.4) FX .042 (1.1)	Suction
General-purpose, stains, lacquer sealers	•	•		705	AV-1239-705	25	8	7 (175)	FF .055 (1.4) FX .042 (1.1) G .028 (.70)	Pressure
Detail, touch-up, stains, lacquer	•			395	EGA-439-395	40	3	6 (150)	E .070 (1.8)	Suction

[1]Low = up to 23 seconds Zahn #2; medium = 23 to 28 seconds Zahn #2; high = 28+ seconds Zahn #2.
Courtesy of ITW DeVilbiss Co.

tip combinations as options. Most good-quality guns do. The tip and cap will come in sets, and the manufacturer will tell you which set is appropriate for thin, medium, or thick finishes, and the size of the spray pattern that will result (see the sample chart above).

If your gun will run off a compressor, make sure the compressor is large enough to supply the gun you choose. Most manufacturers offer a specification sheet that will tell you what volume of air (cfm) the gun will draw throughout the range of pressures (psi) it can handle.

Other Tools

Though we don't use them to apply the finish, the tools in this group are valuable helpers. Some, like masking tape, may even work to keep finish off an area, which can be as important as putting it on. Others, like filters, can save time by reducing the amount of corrective sanding you'll have to do later on. Most of the items in this section will, one way or another, help you get a better finish with fewer problems.

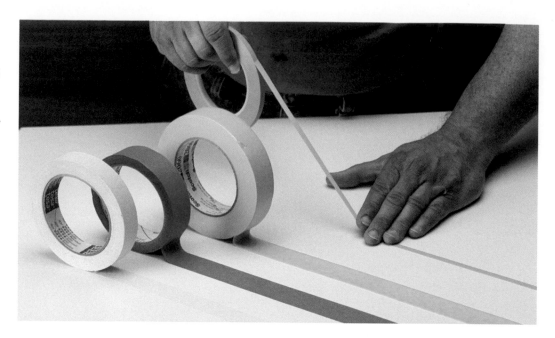

From front to back: common beige masking tape; blue 2090 Long-Mask Masking Tape; green 2060 Lacquer Masking Tape; and Fine Line Tape.

To make the finishing easier, I stained the parts of a bookcase before I put them together. I masked off the areas that will become glue joints to keep the stain off them. When I peeled off the tape, the stain had crept under it and left a ragged line. To make matters worse, the tape kept tearing and left adhesive all over the wood. What did I do wrong?

Some masking tapes use adhesive that will dissolve in the solvents commonly used in stains, and most tape will start to degrade and leave adhesive residue on the wood after a day or so. The 3M Company makes a tape called 2090 Long-Mask Masking Tape designed to peel off clean up to a week after it's applied. It also resists solvent creep better than most, although their 2060 Lacquer Masking Tape is made specifically to leave a clean line. Either 3M tape will give you better results than common masking tape. After you apply the tape, burnish the edge to make sure it is down solidly. Let it sit for an hour or so before you stain. When it is time to remove the tape, peel it back flat over itself and away from the stain line at about 30° and you'll get a cleaner removal than pulling the tape straight upward.

Masking Tape

Masking tape helps isolate an area while you're staining an adjacent section, separate paint colors on multicolored pieces, and keep glue joints clean during "prefinishing," which means finishing furniture parts before you assemble them. Not all masking tape is alike. Listed below are some of the tapes you'll find at the store, along with their relative strengths and weaknesses.

Common beige masking tape allows stains and finishes that contain naphtha, mineral spirits, or lacquer thinner to creep under the adhesive, resulting in a ragged line when you peel off the tape. To make matters worse, the longer you leave the tape on, the harder it is to remove. After just a few days the tape will tear and leave adhesive residue behind when you try to remove it. Use this tape when it will be removed soon and a clean line is not critical.

The correct way to remove masking tape is to pull it back over itself at a 30° angle away from the painted edge.

2090 Long-Mask Masking Tape is a bright blue tape made by 3M Company. It leaves a fairly clean line with most stains and finishes and removes easily, even up to seven days later, so there is no adhesive residue on the wood. Use it to mask raw wood when prefinishing or staining when tape will remain on for more than one day.

2060 Lacquer Masking Tape, another 3M product, is bright green. It resists solvent creep, even lacquer thinner, and leaves a crisp line. Use it for separating different-colored lacquers on two-tone finish jobs or for masking off areas when spraying lacquer. It will leave a crisper line than the blue tape but should not be left on as long.

Fine Line Tape is a flexible tape, also from 3M. It allows you to tape curves without folds or bubbles in the tape. In addition, the tape is only half as thick as

On thick finishes, you may have to score a line first with a razor blade before peeling off the tape.

other tapes, so it leaves a smaller ridge where the finish meets it. Use this tape for masking curves and when you must blend two colors into a smooth surface.

Filters

Once you open a can of finish, airborne particles are bound to get into it. To make matters worse, some coatings, especially waterbornes, create small specks of coagulated finish in the can. To avoid getting

This cleverly designed stand holds both a spray gun and a filter to leave your hands free for pouring finish.

anything other than a smooth coat of wet finish, it is a good idea to strain the finish through a filter before you apply it.

Common cone-shaped filters are available from any store that sells coatings—and often they are free. Straining finish through these filters takes out large particles that might show up on the surface. You can also use lint-free cheesecloth or nylon stockings as filter media. Loosely cover the container you are pouring finish into with the cloth and secure it with a rubber band or tape.

When I'm spraying lacquer, I like to use a "barrel" filter. It fits over the stem of a siphon- or pressure-feed cup and filters the material just before it enters the gun's fluid passage (see the photo on the facing page).

If you spray using a compressor to supply air to the gun, you also need to filter the air you use. An inline air filter or "extractor" will remove any water or oil that has gotten into the air lines, delivering clean air to the spray gun. These filters are available from any store that sells spray equipment, compressors, or air-line hose.

Weighing and Measuring Tools

I often use a scale when I am mixing stains, shellac, and other finishes. Measuring by weight is generally the most accurate way to mix finish materials, and it lets you re-create a color or mixture exactly. Nothing is quite so frustrating as mixing the perfect stain for a job and then running out with just two panels left to do and no way of getting that exact color again. If you take the time to weigh your materials, take the time to write down the formula as well.

To measure how thick a finish has been applied, there is a clever gadget called a wet film thickness gauge (see the photo on p. 42). It has crenelated sides that are ground at different depths and marked in mils (thousandths of an inch). Press the gauge into the wet film and read the finish thickness by seeing which marked tab last touched the finish. Use it in an inconspicuous area on lacquer because it will leave marks. On slow-drying films, like varnish, you can touch it down, read the thickness, and quickly brush out the marks.

Viscosity is the measure of how thin or thick a liquid is. Most spray guns tell you how much pressure to use and what tip to buy based on the viscosity of the finish you will be spraying. A viscosity cup is a small cup on a long vertical handle, like a small ladle, but with a hole at the bottom. You dip the cup into the finish until it is full, lift it up, and count how many seconds it takes to empty completely. Take a look at the chart on p. 37 and you will see viscosity range based on a particular type of cup, the Zahn #2. That and the Ford #4 are the two common cup types used to measure finish viscosities.

Scales are available almost anywhere, but wet thickness gauges and viscosity

A barrel screen sits on the end of the fluid stem and filters the finish before it leaves the gun.

cups are not so common. One reliable source is Paul N. Gardner Co. (316 N.E. First Street, Pompano Beach, FL 33060; 954-946-9454).

Mixing Containers

I know this seems mundane, but mixing containers are another simple but necessary tool. It is always a bad idea to dip a brush directly into a can of coating. By pouring some out into another vessel, you can be certain you only mix what you need and the remaining unused material stays uncontaminated.

Whether I am mixing colors, thinning out varnish, or straining material, I pour it out of its original container and into something more convenient for application. It might be a throwaway aluminum pie plate, a plastic yogurt cup, or a straight-sided enameled pan that I prefer for brushing varnish. Choose the container based on what will go into it and how you will use it. A flat aluminum pan might be just right for loading a rag or paint pad. The enameled pan I use for varnish has straight sides that let me touch off the ends of the bristles so I don't get drips. Avoid plastics when you use strong solvents, like lacquer thinner, and avoid iron containers with any waterborne product (stainless steel is okay). Aluminum is fine for most finishes, except shellac, which can corrode or pit the metal.

3 Stripping

Removing old finish is a messy, labor-intensive job. There is no way to change that, but knowing how best to use the available materials can help. Before you launch into a major stripping project, first make sure that it is necessary and appropriate. Many defects and damages can be repaired and surfaces brightened and renewed without stripping. Even in those cases where you want to change to a darker color, you can often finish over an old coating if it is in good shape and there is no flaking or peeling of the finish. In most cases, it is inappropriate to strip antiques. While there are exceptions, most very old pieces lose value when the original finish is removed. If you are not sure, get the advice of a conservator first.

Once you are certain that stripping is the right course of action, move on to the rest of this chapter. Here you will find the best materials and methods to do the job, along with some advice about removing old stains. As always, I'll help you approach both stripping and cleaning up afterward in a way that is safe and responsible.

Which Method to Use?

The three traditional methods of removing finish are to scrape or sand it off with scrapers or sandpaper, to bubble or burn it off with a torch or heat gun, or to lift it with chemical strippers. Of the three, chemical stripping is the best choice for furniture. Scraping, sanding, and applying heat are appropriate for large areas of exterior woodwork, such as the outside of a house where exterior paint has started to flake and peel. But for indoor work on furniture, chemicals create fewer potential problems.

Choosing a Stripper

The good news is that most strippers remove most finishes. The major exception is a "refinisher," which is only for shellac and lacquer. If you don't know what kind of finish is on the furniture you want to strip, choose any can that says "paint and varnish remover" on the label. Fast or slow, it will most likely do the job. There are a few modern finishes that simply won't budge with anything, but these are fairly rare and are found only on recent pieces of furniture.

Since most strippers will work, you are free to choose a stripper based on its speed and safety (use the chart on p. 47 as a quick reference guide). A good rule of thumb is that the safer a stripper is, the slower it is. The safest stripper available can be used indoors with no special ventilation and no gloves. However, it may take 24 hours to soften a finish. By contrast, nonflammable methylene-chloride-based strippers cut through even multilayer coatings in as little as 10 minutes, but they are not as safe.

In light of this relationship between speed and safety, it makes sense to divide strippers into three groups based on those qualities: fast and hazardous; medium fast and mostly safe; and slow and very safe.

Fast and Hazardous

There are two types of removers in this group; refinishers and methylene-chloride strippers. While methylene-chloride strippers work on virtually any finish, refinishers are not so versatile. They are

Scrapers and sandpaper don't know the difference between paint and wood, and the odds are you will damage or gouge the wood surface with either. Furthermore, scrapers will not take paint out of the pores in woods with large pores without removing large amounts of wood.

Similarly, torches and heat guns will burn finish and scorch wood indiscriminately. They are also likely to start fires, loosen old glue on veneers and in joints, and may create toxic fumes while vaporizing certain components of old paint, such as heavy metals.

Chemicals, of course, are not without their hazards, but with simple precautions they can be quite safe. With the single exception of caustic strippers, chemical strippers will not harm the wood beneath the finish no matter how long they are left on.

Safety First

It's impossible to talk about paint removers without talking about safety. Most paint removers are inherently unsafe, which makes sense if you think about it. You are using a chemical strong enough to destroy a finish that was designed to be strong enough to protect wood, so the chemicals must be powerful.

Some strippers require less protection than others, but it's better to be cautious no matter what the material. Here are some general rules you should follow:

- Protect your body with long sleeves and a solvent-resistant apron.

- Protect your eyes from splashes with goggles.

- Protect your hands with neo-prene gloves. Buy them long and turn back the ends into cuffs, so that when you lift your arms, the stripper drips into the cuff, not onto your arm.

- Protect your lungs by working in good, strong ventilation or outdoors. Make sure you move enough air so that you don't smell fumes, or wear a good respirator.

Some strippers, such as the ones called "refinisher," are highly flammable. If the can says the stripper is flammable, keep sparks and flames away from your work area. If you use a fan that is not explosion-proof, position it so that you are between the fan and the window or door. Have the fan push clean air toward you and the vapors away from both you and the fan. That way you will not be drawing vapor-filled air through a spark-producing fan motor.

Finally, if you have heart disease, you should avoid using any strippers that contain methylene chloride. Inhaling methylene chloride reduces the amount of oxygen in the blood and can trigger an attack in people with heart disease. Even for the healthy, methylene-chloride-based strippers require serious ventilation.

Ventilating Your Work Area

Cross-ventilation allows solvent-laden air to escape the room.

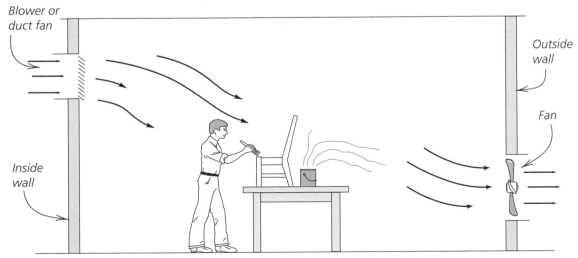

Blower or duct fan

Inside wall

Outside wall

Fan

Fast and hazardous strippers include methylene-chloride-based strippers (left and spray can) and refinishers (right).

Refinisher quickly melts the lacquer on this Martin guitar right down to the bare wood. Refinisher is particularly helpful when you must strip just one area of a shellacked or lacquered piece.

only appropriate for certain types of coatings. Both are hazardous, but for very different reasons.

Refinisher If you know for certain that the finish is either plain lacquer or shellac, you can choose the can that says "refinisher" on the label. Refinisher is a mixture of solvents that will redissolve shellac or lacquer and turn it back into liquid. It will not work on polyurethane, paint, or oil varnishes. Refinisher is flammable, poisonous, and requires good ventilation. It works very fast, and the best method of working with it is different than with all other strippers. Wearing gloves and goggles, soak steel wool or a nylon abrasive pad with refinisher and then scrub the surface of the finished object. The finish will start melting almost immediately as it liquefies, and you can wipe it off. Repeat the process until you are down to bare wood. As soon as the wood is dry, you can refinish.

Methylene-chloride strippers When methylene chloride first came on the scene, it was hailed as a safety miracle. The greatest danger at that time was fire, since most strippers were very flammable. Methylene chloride is so nonflammable that when you add enough of it to other solvents, it makes them nonflammable. For many years, strippers that contain high amounts of methylene chloride have been the standard paint remover in the

Stripper Scorecard

Type of stripper	Identifying it by the label	Speed and efficiency	Appropriate uses	Safety rating
Refinisher	"Contains methanol, acetone, and toluene"	fast top-down stripper; will melt finishes to liquid in layers	lacquer, shellac	flammable, hazardous to inhale and through skin
Methylene chloride (DCM)	"Contains methylene chloride"	the fastest bottom-up stripper; removes finish in sheets	all finishes	nonflammable; hazardous to inhale and through skin
Mid-range solvent mixtures	"No methylene chloride, no caustics" or "Contains n-methyl-2-pyrrolidone" or "Gamma butyrolactone" or "Removes paint in as little as little as 30 minutes"	slower than DCM; generally a top-down stripper	all finishes	usually nonflammable, but still requires gloves, goggles, and some ventilation
Caustic or lye	"Corrosive—causes severe burns" or "Contains calcium hydroxide, (or) sodium hydroxide, (or) magnesium hydroxide, water"	fairly fast top-down stripper	all finishes— even milk paint and wallpaper!	nonflammable, but highly corrosive; requires gloves, goggles, and gentle ventilation
DBE (di-basic ester)	"3M Safest Stripper"	very slow; may take 24 hours; top-down stripper	varnish, paint, all oil-based coatings; less effective on lacquer	quite safe; DBE stripper can be used with no special ventilation

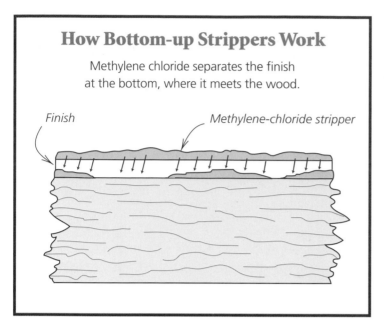

How Bottom-up Strippers Work

Methylene chloride separates the finish at the bottom, where it meets the wood.

Finish

Methylene-chloride stripper

industry. The downside is that inhaling methylene-chloride fumes can cause problems for people with heart conditions, and some suspect that high exposure can cause cancer. For these reasons, it must be used with great care and good ventilation. Read the sidebar on safety precautions carefully (see p. 45) if you choose methylene-chloride strippers.

Methylene chloride (also called dichloromethane, or DCM) is a bottom-up stripper. Once applied, it quickly drops down through the finish, no matter how many layers there are, and starts melting the finish at the bottom, where it meets

Methylene-chloride bottom-up strippers release finishes at the wood line first, allowing some coatings to lift off in sheets.

the wood (see the drawing on the facing page). With DCM strippers, the paint usually comes off in sheets, having been released from the wood before the solvent got a chance to dissolve the entire finish. Therefore, you often use less of this type of stripper than any other because you really only need to make the finish let go, not dissolve it completely. Not only does this make stripping faster and easier, but it also makes cleanup nicer too. The stripper evaporates quickly from the sludge you removed, and the sludge turns back into a pile of dried finish. At that point it is landfill-safe. I'll explain more about that in the clean-up section (see pp. 56-58).

Medium Fast and Mostly Safe

There are two types of strippers in this group: solvent mixtures and caustics. The solvent mixtures are by far the fastest-growing group of strippers. They are the industry's attempt to deal with the unfortunate drawbacks of methylene chloride without losing its speed and versatility. They represent the middle-of-the-road solution in that they tend to be fairly safe and not too slow. In contrast, caustic strippers are fast disappearing from the scene. They don't give off solvent fumes, but they can burn both skin and wood if they are mishandled.

Solvent mixtures When it became clear that DCM was a hazardous ingredient, manufacturers started looking for alternatives and came up with a variety of solvent mixtures that filled their needs.

Here are three of the many "middle of the road" solvent-mixture strippers. Although safer than the fast, hazardous group, these strippers still require gloves and goggles.

If you read the label, you'll notice that some solvent mixtures contain very small amounts of DCM added to other flammable solvents, while others contain a new group of nonflammable solvents such as n-methyl-2-pyrrolidone and gamma butyrolactone. For the moment, these newer solvents appear to be much safer than DCM or even common aromatic solvents, though it is worth noting that all the evidence is not yet in. In spite of their relative safety, these strippers still require gloves, goggles, and some ventilation.

Solvent mixtures are top-down strippers. They melt the finish layer by layer from the top until they reach the wood. For this reason, they take longer to work, and your finish comes off as goo instead of in sheets. They evaporate more slowly

branes, so they must still be handled with care. Some ventilation is needed, and good gloves and goggles are a must.

Caustics are moderately fast. However, they will darken many woods and, if they are left on too long, can even start breaking down the wood itself. While all other strippers can be left on longer than they need to be with no ill effects, caustics cannot. Check the stripper's progress frequently, and when it gets down to the wood level, remove it.

Slow and Very Safe

This is the strangest category of the lot in that it not only contains just one member but is also represented by only one brand: 3M Safest Stripper paint and varnish remover. The 3M Company arrived at their solution to the safety issue far enough ahead of everyone else that they managed to patent it completely. Some eight patents surround their product and protect it sufficiently so that no one else is able to offer anything quite like it, at least until the patents expire. Based on a group of chemicals called di-basic esters (DBE), it is a waterborne stripper that appears to be completely safe. Although gloves are recommended, it does not appear to harm skin, and it gives off no harmful vapors, so no special ventilation is needed. If you must work in a nonventilated area or can't handle harsh chemicals (such as around kids and pets), this is the ticket.

The downside? Safest Stripper is very slow, often taking up to 24 hours to soften a finish. It is a top-down stripper and will

than refinisher or DCM stripper and generate fewer vapors. For many folks, this represents the happy medium—a stripper that is relatively fast yet relatively safe.

Caustics Caustics are strong alkaline solutions, like lye, that will break down most finishes. In fact, these are the only strippers that will remove milk paint. Caustic mixtures are water based, so they are nonflammable and do not fill the air with solvent vapors. However, they are very harmful to skin and mucous mem-

Assemble all your stripping gear before you start.

work on almost any finish. It is particularly effective on oil-based paints and coatings, including polyurethane. Safest Stripper also seems to pull oil-based materials out of the pores of wood better than most anything I have come across. This makes it very handy for woods like oak or ash that have been covered with oil-based enamel, or even for oil spills on wood.

Taking It Off

Now that you have chosen the best stripper for your needs, it is time to make it work for you. Start by creating a work area and gathering up all the tools you will need. Once you are set up, you can put on the stripper, leave the room, and sit back and let the chemical do its work.

When the time is right, you can come back and remove the softened finish. Finally, there will be a scrub-down sequence to make certain the wood is completely clean and some simple procedures to clean up the mess you've created. Take it step-by-step and it will be easier than you think.

Set Up the Work Area

First, clear an area to work in. Having a space where you won't have to worry about banging into things or accidentally getting stripper on a finished surface will let you concentrate on the task at hand. Gather together all the stripping tools you will need before you open any stripper. Once you get your gloves messy, you

Make a tent of polyethylene sheeting for large pieces. The plastic will hold the stripper inside and keep it working longer. Newspaper beneath the table helps keep the floor clean and will catch the removed finish once you untent the piece and start to clean it.

I normally use a liquid paint remover, and it works great. But yesterday my wife asked me to refinish this old plant stand that has about eight coats of paint on it. Will I have to use a paste-type stripper on this?

No. How thick a stripper is has no bearing on its strength. Thick paste strippers are made that way so that they cling to vertical surfaces and don't evaporate as fast. They are not necessarily stronger. In fact, some of the slowest-acting strippers are thick pastes. If you find a thinner liquid easier to work with, and it is strong enough to do the job, stay with it.

won't want to be opening drawers to find things. Here's what you'll need:

- black plastic leaf bags or plastic sheeting
- newspapers
- long neoprene gloves, goggles, a respirator, and an apron
- old cloth or paper towel
- a big sloppy old brush and an empty can or bowl to apply the stripper
- scrub brushes, coarse nylon abrasive pads, a putty knife with the edges rounded
- a sharpened dowel, twine, and some coarse wood shavings for turnings or carvings

Dismantle the piece of furniture as far as is practical and remove all hardware, making certain you label the parts carefully for reassembly. You might want to make a sketch for complicated pieces and number any similar parts in hidden areas, such as inside the joints. You might even want to take "before" photos. It will help during reassembly—and will remind you of how much you've accomplished.

Coat It and Bag It

The key to easy stripping is to get a lot of stripper on and convince it to stay in place for a fairly long time. The most effective way to keep the stripper wet and active for a long time is to seal it in a plastic bag. Do a dry run first, just as you would dry-clamp a complicated setup before putting on the glue. Most small pieces, such as chairs, drawers, and cabinet doors, will fit inside a leaf bag. Just make sure you can close it up with a twist tie. If the piece is too big, like a dining table, headboard, or breakfront, simply make a tent for it of polyethylene sheeting or plastic bags taped together with duct tape, as shown in the photo on the facing page. (The duct tape must be outside the tent, and the plastic overlapped slightly beneath it; otherwise, the stripper will soften the adhesive on the tape.) Make sure the tent goes all the way to the floor, which should also be covered with plastic. I like to put down several layers of newspaper at the bottom of the piece as well.

Once you've done the dry run, unbag the piece and leave the bag rolled up below it. Shake the can of stripper gently by turning it over several times. Drape a cloth or paper towel over the cap and unscrew it slowly. Sometimes a bit of stripper will spurt out, as when you pop the top on a can of soda, so the cloth over the cap will prevent it from spraying on you. Pour some stripper into a metal or glass bowl large enough to dip your brush into.

Daub the stripper on in a thick (⅛-in. to ¼-in.) layer. Thicker, "semi-paste" removers work best on vertical surfaces because they cling better, but other than that, there is no difference between how thin and thick strippers work. Once the stripper is on, leave it alone. Many strippers contain a wax that will rise to the surface and form a crust to prevent the active solvent from evaporating. If you go

Seal smaller pieces, like this chair, in a plastic leaf bag or oversize garbage bag after you have covered it with stripper. The stripper will not melt through the plastic bag.

back and brush the stripper back and forth or move it around after it is on, you will disturb the crust and cause the active ingredients to evaporate faster. As soon as you have the entire piece completely coated, cover it with the bag and seal it up. Now go away (and I mean that in the nicest sort of way). Don't worry about the bag touching the wet stripper—it will not dissolve the plastic. I promise.

Peel back the bag and bunch it up below the piece to act as a drop cloth while you start removing the softened finish.

Strip It

Which stripper you chose and how thick the finish is will dictate how long you must leave the bag sealed. For DCM-based strippers, an hour or two should do it. Leave the medium-fast group on for at least two hours and as long as overnight. 3M's Safest Stripper may need as much as 24 hours in the bag. If you are not sure, put the stripper on late in the day, make sure the bag is well sealed, and simply leave it until morning. Even the fast methylene-chloride strippers can stay on overnight with no ill effects to the wood. However,

A handful of wood shavings helps remove the finish in hard-to-reach areas (left). You can use a stiff bristle brush to clean out the soaked shavings (right).

this method does not work for caustic strippers. They should be checked periodically and the gunk removed as soon as the wood starts to come clean.

When it is time to remove the finish, open the windows, turn on the fan, put on your goggles, apron, respirator, and gloves, and peel back the bag carefully, bunching it up as before. It will now act as your drop cloth and clean-up aid. The finish should come off right down to the bare wood. Scoop it up with a putty knife on flat surfaces, and use stiff-bristle brushes on round or carved areas. I'll

sometimes grab a handful of wood shavings and use them as a free-form scrubber to remove gunk, as shown in the bottom left photo on the facing page. A sharpened dowel will help dislodge gunk in tight corners, and twine gets into tight recesses in turnings (see the photos below).

As you remove the finish gunk, spread it out on newspaper, using as much newspaper as you need. The object is to spread it out and let it dry before you throw it away. More on that later (see pp. 56-58).

You need to remove the finish quickly because if some finish doesn't come off,

A sharpened dowel will help clean finish from tight corners without damaging the wood.

Coarse twine works great for cleaning old finish from the grooves on turned legs.

As you remove the softened finish, spread the gunk onto newspapers. Once it dries to a hard crust, the paint-laden paper will be landfill-safe.

I have some antique furniture that looks like rosewood, but upon closer inspection I realized that the grain is fake. How is this done and with what? If the finish is shot, is it possible to refinish without removing the fake graining?

No, it is not possible to strip the finish without destroying the fake graining. As to how it is done, that would take more space than I have here.

Put simply, a variety of pigments and dyes are manipulated by a variety of feathers, special brushes, graining combs, and other tools to make the wood look like another wood. In short, you paint a picture of rosewood on top of some other wood. It is called *faux bois,* the French for fake wood. The graining is coated with clear finish for protection, but paint stripper will remove it all—the clear coat and the graining.

you'll have to recoat with more stripper before the original coat dries. If that's the case, simply tie up the bag again after recoating and come back tomorrow. That should do it. If the wood starts to dry while you are scrubbing off the last vestiges of finish, add more stripper to your brush or pad to keep the wood wet until all the paint is removed.

Wash It Down

Before the wood has a chance to dry, wash it down to get it really clean. This step will help remove those last bits of paint that keep showing up after you wipe them away and will also remove the wax that the stripper leaves on the wood.

For the solvent wash, mix equal parts of denatured alcohol, mineral spirits, and lacquer thinner. Use a nylon pad or scrub brush to scrub down the wood with the mixture until it is clean and thoroughly wet. Wipe the wood dry with paper towels or clean rags. Now repeat the scrub with a solution of ½ cup of household ammonia in 1 qt. of warm water. The solvent mixture helps remove some alcohol-soluble dye stains, pigmented stains, and waxes. The ammonia wash helps remove any silicone or other oils. This wash is especially important if you plan to refinish with solvent-based or waterborne lacquer. Let the wood dry overnight.

Clean Up

Now that the furniture piece is clean, it is time to clean up the work area. Clean any scrubbers, brushes, gloves, or putty knives

If all the paint does not come off easily, recoat the piece with more stripper and rebag it.

Before the wood has a chance to dry, scrub the surface with solvent to remove any clinging finish residue. This chair gives you an idea of how clean the surface should be before you start the solvent scrub step.

that you want to keep with the remaining solvent-wash liquid. Dump any leftover ammonia mixture down the sink. You should be left with a small amount of solvent mixture, a fairly messy plastic bag, some solvent-laden rags or paper towels, and a lot of newspapers with melted finish gunk on them. Put them all out where they'll get exposed to plenty of fresh air but are away from people and animals, and let them dry out. You can speed the evaporation of the liquid solvent by pouring it into a pile of wood shavings spread out on newspaper or plastic. Wet sludge is hazardous waste and must be disposed of according to your local regulations, which vary from area to area. However, once all the solvents evaporate and the gunk dries

How clean is clean? This chair is down to the raw wood, and its several coats of colored paint are merely a memory. It is now ready to finish.

Spread out the gunk-filled newspaper and solvent-laden rags and towels outside to dry. Make sure they are in an area where they will not get rained on and are away from children and animals.

Laundry bleach will remove dye stains but will not usually change the natural color of the wood or remove most pigmented stains. This cherry board was stained with pigment on the left, with dye on the right, and left natural in the middle. One swipe of bleach completely removed the dye but left the other two sections intact.

to a solid crust, the plastic bag, rags, and finish-laden newspapers are landfill-safe. You can collect them and put them out with the trash.

Removing Old Stain

Even though you have removed all the finish, there may still be stain in the wood from the first time the piece was finished. Whatever pigmented stains and pore filler survived the solvent scrub are likely to be there for good, unless you sand them out. However, there are some methods that work on certain types of stains. Dye stains may be wiped out with laundry bleach; iron stains may come out with oxalic acid; and water rings and ink stains may get lighter with wood bleach.

Using Laundry Bleach

Dye stains can often be bleached successfully with ordinary laundry bleach. (If you're looking for this solution in a woodworking supply house, it will be labeled decolorant or dye neutralizer.) Sand the wood lightly to be certain that all wax or residue is gone. Put on gloves and goggles and scrub the entire piece of furniture with fresh laundry bleach (Chlorox, Purex, etc.) on a nylon abrasive pad or scrub brush. Let the wood dry completely. If there is no change, the stain is probably a pigment. If some, but not all, of the stain comes out, repeat the bleach wash. When it dries, bleach reduces to salt and water. Brush off the salt or sponge it off with clean water.

Bleaches

	Dye stains	Blue-black iron stain	Ink, pigments, watermarks	Lightens wood
Laundry bleach	yes	no	no	no
Oxalic acid	no	yes	some	no
Wood bleach (A/B bleach)	yes	no	some	yes

Using Oxalic Acid

Woods high in tannin, like oak, will stain if they come in contact with iron. Old furniture will often show dark blue-black stains where iron nails or hardware were against the wood. These stains will come out with a wash of oxalic acid.

Oxalic acid is sold as a white crystalline powder in most hardware and home stores. Remove any iron, including any partially hidden nails, from the wood first. Mix about 1 tablespoon of oxalic acid to 1 cup of warm water and flood it on the entire surface, not just where the stain is. Let the wood dry completely. Sponge off the dried crystal residue the next day to leave the wood clean. One application usually removes the iron stain without changing the original color of the wood itself, but difficult stains may take a second wash.

In its dry powdered form, oxalic acid is a toxic irritant to mucous membranes. Handle it carefully, wearing goggles and a dust mask, and wash your hands afterward.

Oxalic acid, often sold as deck brightener, will remove stains caused by iron on woods high in tannin. Mix 1 tablespoon of oxalic acid to 1 cup of warm water.

FINISHING TALES

High Sobriety

We knew Rusty was an alcoholic when we hired him. But he insisted that all he needed to stay off the sauce was a good job. He drank because he had nothing to do but sit home all day and, well...drink.

Like all new employees, he was assigned to "finisher's hell"—the strip tank. There you had to stand all day over a vat full of smelly chemicals stripping finish off furniture. The strange thing was, he actually seemed to enjoy it. He was happy back there. Every day he showed up on time and cheerfully dove into the nastiest job in the shop. And he managed to stay sober to boot. He even had a favorite stripper, a mysterious blend the vendor called "cool strip." It was designed as an inexpensive post-remover wash-off thinner, but Rusty discovered that it would quickly remove both shellac and lacquer finishes by itself, and most of the stuff we stripped was lacquer.

All that ended with the infamous "oak" coffee table. Rusty popped it into the strip tank and started in on it. A few minutes later he was back in the main room, clearly agitated, with eyes as big as saucers. "You've gotta come see this," he stammered, "I don't know what I did, but the boss is gonna kill me."

Wherever the cool strip had hit the "oak" table, the "oak" was gone. Instead of stripped oak, there was plain, ugly poplar. The table had a printed finish, where a photograph of fancy wood grain is printed directly onto cheap, plain wood. As the clear topcoat was removed, so was the beautiful oak pattern the owner loved. One of the younger workers spoke first. "Uhhmmm, what happened to the wood grain?" he asked. Rusty just moaned.

He never showed up for work the next day. Or the next. Jimmy the Hacker went to his apartment and reported back. "He's gone. Fell off the wagon. Crawled back into the bottle. We'll never see him in here again." And we never did. "Strange, though," continued Jimmy, "he says he never missed the booze as long as he was working the strip tank. Must be the fumes. Go figure!"

Two days later, Tony came to deliver more cool strip and pick up the empty 55-gallon drum. I walked him out to his truck.

"Hey, Tony," I asked, "what's in that stuff anyway? Mostly lacquer thinner?" "Nah," he replied, "mostly alcohol. Why do you ask?"

I shrugged. "No reason." I turned and walked back inside.

Using Wood Bleach

Other accidental stains, like water rings and ink, will resist chlorine bleach and oxalic acid but may come out with wood bleach or "A/B bleach." Wood bleach is sold as a set of two bottles, one containing lye and the other hydrogen peroxide. Both are very caustic and should be handled carefully with gloves and goggles in place.

The directions may say to mix the two, but more commonly they suggest applying one liquid, followed quickly by the second. In either case, the object is to have the two chemicals come in contact with

Two-part wood bleach actually lightens the wood itself. The effects are obvious on these pieces of maple (top), walnut (center), and mahogany (bottom).

the wood while both are still wet. The reaction of the two chemicals will bleach the wood, taking out many accidental stains in the process. However, it will also remove the original color of the wood, leaving woods like walnut looking more like butternut.

Use a nylon pad, rag, or synthetic bristle brush to flood the two chemicals onto the entire surface of the piece quickly. Bleaching just one area will result in water marks. Let the wood dry overnight. Repeat the process to lighten it even further. When the wood is dry, neutralize the surface by sponging it off with plenty of clean water.

All bleaches contain water and may leave the surface of the wood rough. After bleaching, you will need to sand the surface lightly with 220-grit sandpaper to smooth it again.

After three attempts, I'm ready to give up. I tried bleaching a walnut mantel with Chlorox in order to lighten it to the color of butternut. It just won't get light enough, even after several attempts. Each time I wetted the wood down and left it to sit overnight. What am I doing wrong?

You are using the wrong bleach. Chlorine bleach (Chlorox) works great to remove dye stains but will not change the natural color of wood. To lighten wood, you need wood bleach. It is sold in most home, paint, and hardware stores. Wood bleach comes as a set of two bottles, one containing lye and the other peroxide. Put the first one on the wood and follow with the second while the wood is still wet from the first. The reaction of the two chemicals will bleach out the natural color of the wood. Both chemicals, and the two together, are caustic, so be certain to wear goggles, gloves, and protective clothing.

4 Preparing the Wood

Finish is thin and revealing. If the surface of the wood has any dents, gouges, or scratches, or is uneven, it will show up in the finish, so good preparation is critical to good finishing. Once the surface is level, it has to be made uniform. The best way to do that is to sand all of the wood in the same way with the same sandpaper. Understanding the differences between abrasive materials and the best ways to use them will make this chore less arduous. Finally, if you plan to use any waterborne stains or finishes, it is a good idea to raise the grain of the wood first.

Fixing Dents and Gouges

A dent is an indentation in wood where the fibers have been crushed, but not broken, cut, or removed. If the wood fibers have been cut or if wood has been removed, then the void is called a gouge. Dents on raw wood can usually be fixed by steaming them out, either with water or with alcohol (see the photos on the facing page).

If you use water, place a few drops into the dent and let the water sink in for a few seconds. With a damp cloth over the spot to protect the wood from scorching, place a hot iron over the dent and hold it there for several seconds. As the iron heats the water, it converts to steam, expanding the crushed fibers in the process. Repeat the process if the dent does not come out completely the first time.

The sequence is a bit different with alcohol. With a small brush or toothpick, place a drop of denatured alcohol into the dent. Now touch a lit match to the alcohol, and it will burn with an almost invis-

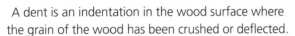

Dents and Gouges

Dent

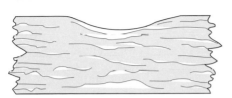

A dent is an indentation in the wood surface where the grain of the wood has been crushed or deflected.

Gouge

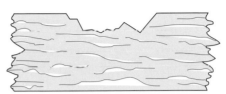

A gouge is an indentation in the wood surface where the grain of the wood has been torn or broken.

Lifting Dents

With water

1 With the wood horizontal, place several drops of water into the dent.

2 Cover the spot with a slightly damp cloth and place a hot knife or iron directly over the drop. Hold it there, checking frequently, until the spot is dry. If the dent is not completely out, repeat the process.

With alcohol

1 To raise a dent with alcohol instead of water, place one drop of denatured alcohol into the depression with a fine touch-up brush or toothpick.

2 Touch the drop with the tip of a lit match. The alcohol will burn with an almost imperceptible blue flame. It will expand rapidly as it burns, causing the crushed wood in the dent to swell.

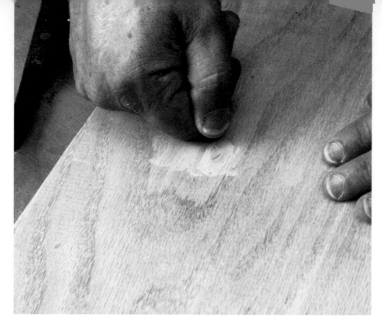

Putty will shrink as it hardens, so let it protrude slightly above the surrounding surface. The putty is ready to sand when it will not take an impression from your thumbnail.

Sand until the original shape of the gouge is clearly outlined.

ible flame. Once again, the heat expands the crushed fibers. The alcohol will go out within a couple of seconds and will not have time to scorch the surrounding wood. Be certain you stick to one drop of alcohol at a time to prevent scorching, and keep some water handy just in case.

In most cases, the raised dent will be level enough so that just a small amount of sanding will erase it completely. However, if the dent does not come out completely, you should treat it as if it were a gouge.

Gouges have to be filled with some type of wood putty to bring them level with the surrounding wood. Press the putty into the gouge so that it is slightly higher than the rest of the surface. The putty will shrink as it dries, so adjust the amount of excess accordingly. To test the putty's dryness, insert your thumbnail (see the top photo at left). If the putty gives, let it dry some more. If the putty is hard and dry, you can sand the spot smooth and level to the rest of the surface.

There are many different brands and types of putty on the market, but most fall into one of three categories: waterborne or "latex" putty, solvent-based putty, and dry powders that will mix with water to form putty. These wood putties dry hard and can be sanded flat once they are dry. They should not be confused with "oil putty," used for filling nail holes in finished molding, or "glazier's putty," used for setting panes of glass. Those two putties do not dry hard but stay flexible indefinitely. They will not work for filling gouges.

Solvent-based putty (front center) dries faster than waterborne "latex" putty (left). The putty to the right is sold in powdered form and must be mixed with water.

What is the difference between wood putty, wood filler, and pore filler? I see all these names in the store and never know which to buy.

The main difference is the thickness of the material. Wood putty and wood filler are two names for thick mixtures of resin, pigment, and wood dust or mineral powder designed to fill nicks, gouges, and voids in wood. They are meant to be pressed into voids in raw wood and sanded smooth once they are dry.

Pore filler is merely a slightly thinner version of the same thing, designed to fill pores in open-pore woods, such as mahogany and walnut. It is formulated to dry fast in thin applications and to rub off easily. However, in a pinch, it is certainly acceptable to thin out your favorite wood putty and use it as a pore filler.

No matter which of the three types of hard-drying putty you choose, they all work in the same way. Some may take stain better than others, and some may dry a bit faster, but you use them in the same way: by filling the gouge slightly proud and sanding the spot flush once it is dry.

Wood putties also come in a wide range of colors. However, you'll notice that no matter how many colors the store has, there is no guarantee that one will match your wood. Fortunately, all types of putty can be colored to match your repair. Dry pigment powders, sold as touch-up colors, artist's fresco powders, or cement colors, work for all types of putty. Mix the color you need by adding the powders a little at a time. If the putty starts to get too thick, add a few drops of the appropriate solvent.

If you can't find a putty that matches the wood, mix a custom color from "natural" putty and cement colors from your local hardware or home store, touch-up powders from wood specialty stores, or artist's fresco powders. If the putty starts to get too thick, add a few drops of the thinning solvent listed on the container.

Sanding

Sanding is tedious. Therefore, your goal is to get the surface smooth enough to finish as quickly as possible. You can save time, energy, and even sandpaper if you use the right sandpaper at each step of the process coupled with an efficient sanding schedule. A good sanding schedule will tell you when to switch from one grit to the next, how to sand in order to remove material quickly and maintain a flat surface, and when to stop sanding.

Types of Sandpaper

Sandpaper is made by gluing pieces of mineral, or "grit," onto a flat backing. The backing can be paper, polyester, cloth, or fiber. Most sandpaper made for hand sanding is paper backed. Various sizes of grit are glued onto the backing with two coats of adhesive, the make coat and the size coat, which work together to hold the grit in place (see the drawing below). Changing the type of paper and adhesive gives us many different types of papers designed for a variety of uses. For example, wet/dry sandpaper, designed to work with a liquid lubricant, is made with waterproof paper and adhesive.

Similarly, different types of mineral are used for grit. Some grits work best for sanding metals and plastic, while others are ideal for wood. The type of grit, along with how it is positioned on the paper, will determine which jobs the sandpaper does best.

Sandpaper is sold in grit "sizes" to indicate how rough or fine it is. Unfortunately, there are at least four common grading systems that companies use to indicate grit size, and they bear little resemblance to one another. They are CAMI, the US standard; FEPA, the European standard; micron grading, a more accurate system used for fine grits; and generic names like "fine," "medium," and so on. As a result, one number size of sandpaper may be entirely different from the same number size of another grading type. For example, 500 grit CAMI is equal to 1,000 grit on the FEPA scale and 19 on the micron scale (see the chart on the facing page).

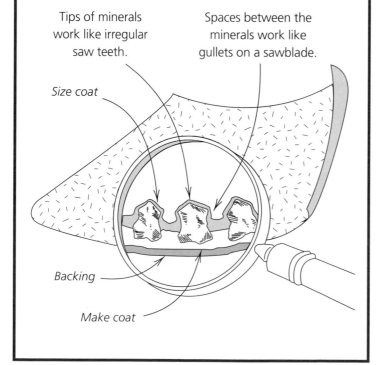

Anatomy of Sandpaper

Sandpaper has pieces of "grit," actually types of stone, glued to a backing made of paper, cloth, or polyester with two layers of adhesive—a make coat and a size coat.

Tips of minerals work like irregular saw teeth.

Spaces between the minerals work like gullets on a sawblade.

Size coat

Backing

Make coat

Abrasive Grading Systems

CAMI (ANSI)	FEPA	Micron	Generic
1500		3	micro fine
		5	
		6	
1200			
		9	
1000			
		12	
800			ultra fine
		15	
600	P1200		
500	P1000		
		20	
400	P800		super fine
		25	
360	P600		
		30	
	P500		
320	P400	35	extra fine
		40	
	P360		
280		45	
	P320		
		50	
240	P280		very fine
		55	
		60	
220	P220	65	
180	P180		
150	P150		
120	P120		fine
100	P100		
80	P80		medium
60	P60		
50	P50		coarse
40	P40		
36	P36		extra coarse

The four systems use indicators beside the number to let you know which system is applicable. Here's how they look:

- CAMI uses plain numbers—220
- FEPA uses a "P" in front of the number—P220
- Micron uses a Greek letter "mu" behind the number—60μ
- Generic names use words—very fine

Types of grit Aluminum oxide is the most commonly used grit in woodworking sandpaper. It is cheap and there are many different grades for a variety of uses; but it's most significant advantage is that it is friable. That means that as the grit wears, instead of getting dull it fractures. The fracture creates a new sharp edge. This friability makes aluminum oxide stay sharp longer, and it results in a paper that keeps sanding quickly and aggressively throughout its life.

Silicon-carbide grit is sharp and tough. While it is technically friable, it will not crack as easily as aluminum

---

The sandpaper I buy for sanding raw wood says "production" on the back. Does that mean it is meant for commercial clients or that it sands fast?

Neither really. "Production" is 3M Company's code word to mean that the paper is made with aluminum-oxide grit. Incidentally, you have made a wise choice for the job. Aluminum-oxide open-coat sandpaper (production paper) is perfect for sanding raw wood. It is sharp, sands fast, and the friable grit keeps sanding efficiently for a long time.

Friable vs. Nonfriable Grit

By cracking and flaking, friable grits present a consistently sharp edge to the wood.

Fracture creates a sharp edge.

Friable

Grit dulls as it wears.

Nonfriable

Types of Grit

	Trade names	Description	Uses
Aluminum oxide	Adalox, Aloxite Imperial, Metalite, Production, Three-M-ite	tough, friable, sharp; the most common and most economical grit	the best grit for sanding raw wood
Silicon carbide	Durite, Fastcut, Powerkut, Tri-M-ite Wet-or-dry	tough, hard, sharp, not easily friable	best for sanding finishes, plastic, metal
Garnet	none	nonfriable, dulls quickly, slow-cutting, burnishes wood	the best grit for final hand sanding of raw wood
Ceramic	Dynakut, Norzon Regalite	very tough, nonfriable	belt sanders and disk sanders (machine sanding)

(Photos by Strother Purdy.)

Open- vs. Closed-Coat Grit

Grit covers 100% of the surface on closed-coat sandpaper
but only 40% to 70% of the surface on open-coat paper.

Open coat
Open coat is best for wood and finish.

Grit acts like a
tiny saw tooth.

Spaces between the grits act like
the gullets between the teeth.

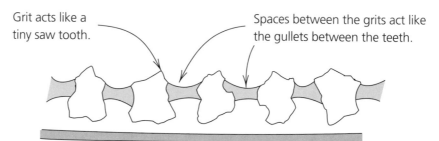

Closed coat
Closed coat is used for sanding metal.

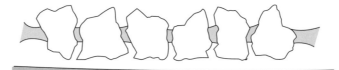

oxide, and wood is generally too soft to make it fracture. Most silicon-carbide grit is used for sanding metal and plastics, including finishes, but not for raw wood. It will work on wood but is somewhat more expensive.

By contrast, garnet is nonfriable, so the grit gets dull as you use it. This too can be an advantage. Though it is less cost-effective and sands slower, nonfriable is ideal to use for the final sanding. Worn garnet leaves a softer U-shaped scratch than the V-shaped scratches left by sharp friable grits. The result is more uniform staining and the ability to burnish end grain so that it is less likely to drink in excessive amounts of stain and finish.

Ceramic grit, which is also nonfriable, is much harder and not as sharp as the other grits. Though it does not get dull quickly, it takes more energy to cut wood. For that reason, it is used mainly for heavy-duty sanding with power tools, like belt sanders and stationary disk sanders.

Stearated sandpaper is best for sanding finishes because it is self-lubricating and doesn't clump.

Closed coat vs. open coat Sandpaper is made in two different coating formats: closed coat and open coat. Closed-coat sandpaper has grit covering the entire surface with no spaces in between the grit particles. Open-coat sandpaper has grit covering only 40% to 70% of the surface and has spaces between the grit (see the drawing on the facing page). If you think of the grit acting like a tiny saw tooth, then the open spaces in between act like the gullets between the saw teeth. That clearance is necessary for sanding both wood and finish, so woodworkers use only open-coat sandpapers. Closed-coat sandpaper, with no space for the sanding swarf to go, would clog up too fast to be effective on raw wood.

Stearated sandpaper Sanding wood generates dry wood dust or "swarf." When you sand finishes, the result is often a fairly sticky residue that clumps onto the sandpaper, rendering it useless. To prevent this clumping, manufacturers lace finish sanding paper with zinc stearate, a white "soap." These stearates lubricate the paper, making it grab less, and prevent sanded finish dust from sticking to the paper. Stearated papers are often referred to as "self-lube" or "lubricated" sandpaper and are lighter in color.

I buy stearated silicon-carbide sandpaper at the local auto paint store. I have been using it to sand raw wood, but my friend says it is the wrong paper for that. I have not noticed any problems. Am I heading for trouble?

Only financial trouble. Stearated silicon-carbide paper will work fine for sanding raw wood, but it is far more expensive than other papers that will work just as well. The paper you are buying is designed for sanding hard finishes and metal, which is why the auto paint store is selling it. If you switch to open coat, nonstearated aluminum-oxide paper for sanding raw wood, it will work just as well and will cost less than half of what you are currently paying. Save the stearated paper for sanding between coats of finish, where you really need it.

The author's favorite sanding block is lined with ¼-in.-thick cork and is sized to fit his hand comfortably.

Wet/dry sandpaper If you attach grit with a waterproof glue onto waterproof paper or polyester, you have wet/dry sandpaper. This paper lets you sand with a liquid as a lubricant, a common way to sand finish in very fine grits. Most wet/dry papers are made with silicon-carbide grit, which is tougher and less friable than aluminum oxide. It is just right for sanding hard finishes.

The Sanding Process

The sanding process is simpler than it seems and really has only two goals. The goal of the first step is to get the wood flat or level while removing any glue spots or machine marks. Every step after that is meant to remove the scratches that were put in during the first step. When you are done, you should have a uniform scratch pattern that will accept stain and finish evenly. It is important that the entire piece be sanded to the same grit; otherwise, the stain will not go on evenly.

Except for the very last step, it makes no difference whether you sand by hand or with a random-orbit sander. The only scratches that will not be eliminated are the last ones put in by the hand-sanding step. If you have it, use a random-orbit sander for all the steps listed except the last one. If not, use a sanding block, following the same steps with the same size and type of grit.

Some woodworkers prefer to use a scraper to smooth the surface of the wood. If you like, you can replace all but

Pressing down on a random-orbit sander will slow its progress and will leave scratches in the wood. Let the weight of the sander alone do the work.

Swirls in the wood are caused by pushing down on the sander.

step #4 with a scraper, but that last hand sanding should still be done as described. Scraped surfaces, especially on dense woods like maple, do not take stain well.

Step 1: 80-grit aluminum oxide
Aluminum-oxide grit will present a sharp edge to remove wood quickly and will stay sharp longer as you work. For a random-orbit sander, you'll need a fairly stiff pad. Soft pads won't support the

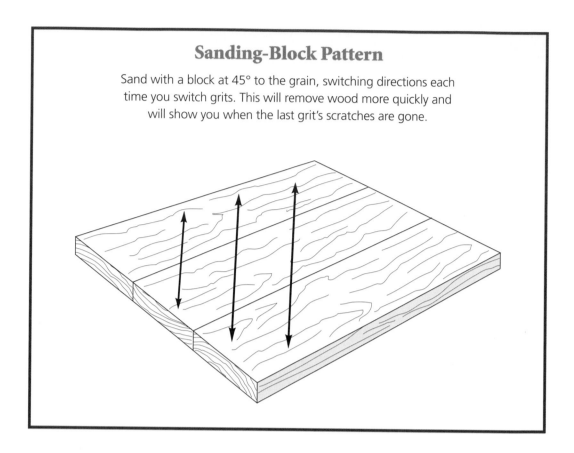

Sanding-Block Pattern

Sand with a block at 45° to the grain, switching directions each time you switch grits. This will remove wood more quickly and will show you when the last grit's scratches are gone.

sandpaper and make it cut more slowly. Move the sander only about 1 ft. every 10 seconds. If you sand by hand, use a sanding block and move it diagonally across the grain at about 45°, as shown in the drawing above. Sanding diagonally removes more wood faster, and the scratches you form will be removed later anyway.

Step 2: 120-grit aluminum oxide

Use 120-grit aluminum oxide until all of the 80-grit scratches are gone. If you use a sanding block, sand at 45° in the opposite direction from the 80-grit sanding to make it easier to see when the 80-grit scratches are gone. If you are using a random-orbit sander, there is no way to

change direction, so you will have to look for wayward scratches a bit more carefully.

Step 3: 180-grit aluminum oxide

As in the previous step, reverse direction and sand until all the 120-grit scratches are gone. Once again, sanding with a random-orbit sander means you have to look carefully for scratches.

Step #4: 180-grit garnet

You should abandon the sander at this step. Sand only by hand and with the grain, not diagonally. Notice that you change types of grit and direction of sanding, but not the grit size. The object here is to straighten out the last scratches

Both sides of this board were sanded with 150-grit paper, the top half with garnet and the bottom half with an aluminum-oxide grit. Pigmented stain shows that the garnet grit leaves wood smoother than the same grit size of aluminum oxide. (Photo by Strother Purdy.)

so they go the same direction as the grain. Garnet grit dulls more quickly than aluminum oxide and will leave a smoother surface that will take stain more evenly. If you don't have garnet paper, do this step with 220-grit aluminum oxide.

Raising the Grain

If you put water on smooth raw wood and then let it dry, you will notice that it will become slightly rough. This is known as "raising the grain" because it makes the ends of the wood fibers stand up (see the drawing on p. 76). Because water will raise the grain, like it or not, it is a good idea to do this intentionally if you plan to use a waterborne stain or coating later in the finishing process.

After the wood has been sanded, take a clean sponge and wet the entire surface of the wood thoroughly with water. Wipe off any excess so that there are no puddles or spots and the wood is uniformly wet. Let it dry overnight. In the morning, use 220-grit paper to scuff-sand the raised "fur" off, applying very light pressure in the direction of the

FINISHING TALES

Rain, Rain Go Away

I had been working for several weeks in a large shop that did no woodworking, only finishing. That morning, a shipment of unfinished Louis XIV chairs was delivered in the rain. Although the truck got close to the loading dock, the 3-ft. gap was enough to dot the chairs with a few raindrops as they were carried over the threshold. Someone called out, "Rain delivery," and by the time the freight elevator got to our third-floor shop, the entire crew was grabbing buckets of water and lots of sponges and rags. To the trucker's (and my) utter amazement, as each chair was brought off the elevator it was frantically washed from top to toe with water, then passed into the workroom, where the water was leisurely wiped off with a dry rag. The evenly damp chairs were then left to dry, as everyone returned to his or her work.

What appeared to the casual observer to be a rehearsal for a Mack Sennett comedy was actually a vital precaution. Water spots are the finisher's nemesis, causing one of the most difficult stains to remove. However, an even wash of water over the entire surface of wood leaves no marks at all. The marks occur primarily at the edge of puddles or single drops; if the wet wood dries evenly, there will be no stains. In order to prevent the raindrops from becoming a problem, the finishers had simply incorporated them into the washdown, before they dried as drops. That way, the worst they could do was contribute to a small amount of grain raising. Since the chairs were to be sanded anyway, the grain raising was not a problem, but water marks would have been a disaster under a clear finish, even if a dark wood stain was used.

Raised Grain

Water "raises the grain" of wood, making the fibers stand up and feel rough.

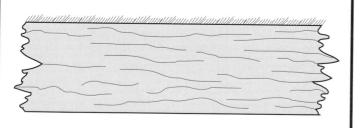

grain. The object is the same as when you shave—remove the raised hairs but don't cut into the surface below. It should take less than 60 seconds to scuff-sand a surface the size of a dining-room tabletop. Once the grain has been raised and scuffed, it will not raise again unless you resand the wood more aggressively with coarser paper.

Coloring Wood

You can color wood in three ways: by staining it, by mixing color into the finish, or by floating color between layers of finish. When you put color directly onto raw wood it is called a stain. If you mix it into the finish, it is known as tinting or shading, and when it is floated between layers of finish it is a glaze. But no matter what layer you add the color to, you will be using the same group of materials. In other words, the same colored liquid we call glaze when it is applied to sealed wood is called stain when applied to raw wood.

For that reason, it makes sense to talk about each of the different coloring materials we have at our disposal and some of the many ways to use them. The most common way to color wood is with stain, so I've started by defining stain, its components, and how each type of stain looks on wood. Included with that is an explanation of commercial stains, those that you find on the paint store shelves, and how to use them. Beyond that is a peek at the many types of specialty stains available to you, how to mix them, and how to apply each one. By the end of the chapter you will have a large arsenal of coloring tools and techniques at your disposal.

What Is Stain?

A stain is anything that adds color to raw wood. Most stains are manufactured colored liquids or gels, but coffee, tea, and berry juice can also be stains, provided they are used on raw wood.

Most stain consists of colorant mixed with a vehicle, a liquid or gel that lets you spread the color evenly onto wood. There are two different types of colorants (dyes

Staining wood can change its color and intensify its grain characteristics at the same time.

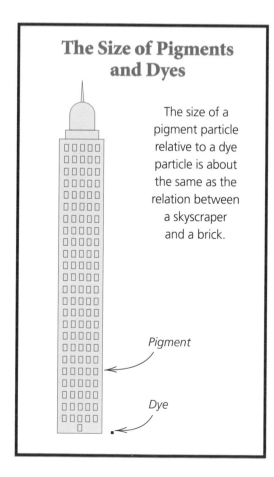

The Size of Pigments and Dyes

The size of a pigment particle relative to a dye particle is about the same as the relation between a skyscraper and a brick.

Pigment

Dye

and pigments) and two types of vehicles (with and without binder). Because these ingredients act differently on wood, it is worth understanding the differences. And it's helpful to know what's in the stains you buy premixed at the store.

Colorants

Colorants are either dyes or pigments or a combination of the two. Dyes are colors that dissolve in some liquid. Once they dissolve, the color particles are extremely tiny—the size of a molecule—so the dye is translucent. Because dye particles are so small, they are absorbed into the wood. Dyes do not settle to the bottom of the container but stay in solution once they are dissolved.

Pigments are ground-up particles of colored dirt. They do not dissolve but instead are suspended in the vehicle. These particles are vastly larger than dye molecules, so they will eventually settle to the bottom of the container if the vehicle is a liquid. You must stir them before you use them.

Dyes and pigments color wood differently. Dyes impart strong, uniform color, even on tight-grained woods like maple. They tend to enhance subtle figure, such as the curl in figured maple. On woods like oak or ash, which have strong grain patterns formed by large pores, the dye makes these patterns less obvious by coloring the background wood as intensely as the grain.

Dyes dissolve in a liquid and will not settle out, as shown in the large glass jar (center). Pigments are relatively large chunks of ground-up colored solids suspended in a liquid; they settle to the bottom of the stains, like those in the three small bottles at left.

How Dyes and Pigments Work

Dye is absorbed by the wood. Pigments sit on top of the wood or settle into the nooks and crannies.

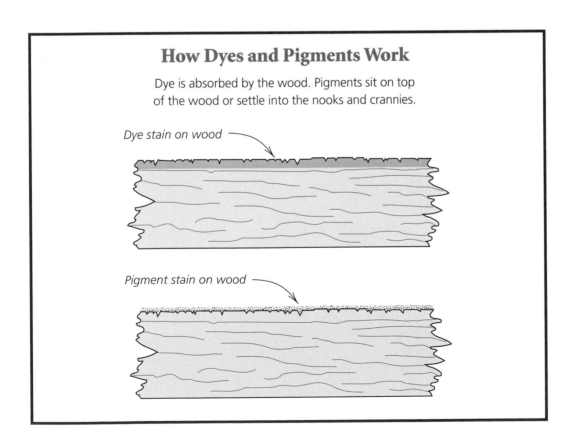

Dye stain on wood

Pigment stain on wood

These oak (left) and maple (right) boards were stained with the same color of dye and pigment and clearly show the differences between the two types of stain. The pigment stain (top half of each board) added color mainly to the large pores that make up the grain pattern of the oak but almost no color to the maple board. The dye (bottom half of each board) made the oak much darker and more uniform, almost hiding the large grain pattern, but actually enhanced the curly figure in the maple board, as well as making it much darker.

I've been trying to stain a maple table, but I can't get the color as dark as I'd like. When I wipe off the stain, it all comes back off. What can I do?

Maple is a dense, close-pore wood, so pigmented stains have no place to lodge and wipe back off. To get a deep, dark color, you should switch to a water-soluble dye. Unlike pigments, which sit on top of wood and lodge only where there are pores or recesses, dyes penetrate into the wood. You control how rich the stain is by how you mix it, not by how you apply it. By mixing more dye powder or concentrate into a smaller amount of water, you will make a more intense stain.

Pigments, on the other hand, wipe right off of dense maple, leaving very little color at all. In fact, if too much pigment is left on, the stain may even hide the more subtle figure. On large-pore ash or oak, the pigment concentrates in the grain lines, making them stand out, but does not add as much color to the less porous areas in between (see the photo at left). As a result, pigments create more contrast on woods with large pores in a pronounced grain pattern. Whether pigment or dye or a combination of the two is your best choice depends on the wood and how you want it to look.

Vehicles

Colorants have to be mixed into some liquid so that they are easier to spread. That liquid is called the vehicle. It can be very simple, like pure water in which a dye is dissolved, or more complex, such as the thin varnish used for a combination "stain and sealer." Vehicles fall into two categories: those that are pure solvent and those that contain a binder. The binder acts like glue to hold or bind the pigment to the wood. Almost all of the stains you buy at the hardware store contain binder.

Only dyes can be mixed with a pure solvent, such as water or alcohol, and the result, with nothing else added, is a stain. This type of dye stain can only go on raw wood, not on sealed wood. The color can be changed or even removed at any time, even after it is dry, up until finish is applied over it. Once the solvent evaporates, nothing but dye color is left on the

FINISHING TALES

Surprise—Metamerism!

"Biedermeier cherry," she announced with conviction. "That's the color I want. Biedermeier cherry."

Although Suzette was one of the most exacting decorators we had to work with, I rather enjoyed it when she brought us finishing jobs. At the time, I was the foreman of a four-man "daylight" shop: a cavernous cinderblock garage whose huge door let in copious amounts of bright south Florida sun. As finishers, we were especially boastful of how our "natural" light let us hit colors so well. On that day, though, it wasn't much help.

"But Biedermeier is a style of furniture, not a color," I complained. The truth was, I had no idea what she wanted.

The next morning, she was back, this time with a sample. The small wood block had a rich, warm brown finish, and I quickly promised to match it perfectly.

Three weeks later, the large sideboard gleamed in its finished glory, and I proudly called on Suzette to grant her approval of the work. We positioned the piece by the big open door to show it in its best light. It was to be delivered the next morning. Suzette breezed in at quarter to five and held the sample block next to our finish.

"Perfect!" she announced. "Send it." In ten minutes we had it inside the waiting delivery van, pleased with ourselves for a job well done. The pleasure was short-lived. By ten the next morning, the sideboard had made its way back into the shop, with a furious Suzette close behind.

"What did you do to my sideboard?" she demanded. "Why did you change the color?" I was dumbstruck. We all gathered around as she plopped the sample angrily on top of the buffet.

For half a minute, there was dead silence. "It looks fine to me," I said quietly, and when I turned and saw Suzette's startled face, I realized that it looked fine to her, too. In embarrassed silence, we once again loaded the piece onto the truck.

Half an hour later someone from the front office handed me a slip of paper, saying, "Suzette wants you to come to this address right away."

As I strode into the room I saw the problem immediately. Sitting beneath a bank of incandescent spotlights, the sideboard stood out like a sore thumb—not the rich hue of the sample, but an almost garish orange. Sitting atop the piece was the sample block, its soft brown color giving mute testimony to the disaster.

Without ever having heard the word, we had our first run-in with metamerism, the strange property that causes colored objects that look identical under one set of lighting conditions to appear different under a different light source. When viewed in daylight, the sample and the sideboard were a match; but under the yellow glare of the spotlights, they weren't even close. Apparently, whoever had made that sample had used a different set of coloring media, and the result was a metameric mismatch.

The incident reminded me of the make-up mirror in my cousin's dressing room. Around its frame sat three rows of lights, each slightly different. By changing the lighting tint, she could make sure the eye shadow that perfectly complemented her dress in the daylight would still look good under indoor lighting come evening. Whoever designed her dressing-room vanity must have had a good understanding of both fashion-conscious women and metamerism.

And what of the sideboard? We refinished it, of course. But this time, we closed the big garage door and worked under a set of spotlights set up just for the occasion.

Some stains contain only dye (right) and some contain only pigment (left), but most are combination stains, containing a mixture of both dye and pigment (center).

wood. In other words, even though the wood is now colored, it is still unsealed (raw). For that reason, these solvent-and-dye mixtures can go under any finish. Some examples currently on the market are Clearwater Color Company stains (gel dye in water), Behlen's Solar Lux stain (liquid dye in chemical solvent), and Homestead TransTint Concentrates (concentrated liquid dye in chemical solvent).

Pigments must have some sort of binder that acts like glue to hold them onto the wood. Most vehicles contain a binder, usually in addition to some sol-vent. Dyes will work with either pure solvent or solvent and binder, but pigments *must* have a binder to work. The binder can be almost any finishing resin. Water-borne pigmented stains, for example, are usually in an acrylic or oil emulsion. But by far the most common type of binder for commercial stains is simple linseed oil.

Once the binder in the stain dries, it becomes a very thin sealer for the wood. Therefore, the finish you put on top of the stain must be able to adhere to the binder in it. For example, some waterborne coat-ings may not adhere well to certain oil-based stains. Stains with binder cannot be easily removed or modified after they have dried. Drying time can be from two hours to overnight, depending on the binder used. With the exception of the three stains listed earlier, *all* other stains that you will find on the paint store shelf contain some sort of binder.

Commercial Stains

The stain you buy at the local hardware, paint, or home store is usually oil based and contains either dye, pigment, or a combination of pigment and dye. (Sometimes the labels identify an all-pigment stain, and sometimes they don't.) Dyes tend to color uniformly, whereas pigments tend to highlight large pores in wood. By combining the two into one stain, manufacturers give you a stain that offers the best of both. These combination stains color even dense woods and highlight grain, too.

The best way to use commercial stains, whether they contain dye, pigment, or both, is to apply them with a brush, rag, or nylon pad and wipe off all the excess before the stain dries (see the top two photos on p. 84). This method will give you the most even and uniform coloration.

If you have an artistic bent, you can manipulate pigmented or combination stains to provide highlights and contrast. After you brush or wipe on the stain, selectively remove some, leaving thicker stain in the low areas of the piece being

Help! I stained some cherry and it came out splotchy. Fortunately, it was on a sample, not the table itself. But how do I make the stain come out evenly on the table?

The short answer is to use wood conditioner, but you should understand why it happened so you can avoid it entirely in the future.

Oil-based stains, like the ones you buy at the hardware store, contain a solvent that softens the resin in some types of wood, like cherry and most softwoods. If that stain also has dye in it, and many commercial stains do, the softened resin in the wood absorbs more of the dye than the surrounding areas. This happens primarily with oil- or solvent-based stains with dye in them. Stain with only pigment usually won't do this, nor will water-based dyes. You can avoid the problem by choosing a water-soluble dye or an all-pigment stain.

The premixed oil-based stains at the home store (like Minwax) often contain both pigment and dye, though. With these, you must first pretreat "splotchy" woods with wood conditioner. It is sold in the same section of the store as the stain. Flood the conditioner on and wipe it off. Then stain *before* the conditioner dries completely, and it will stain evenly.

Do not use wood conditioner with any water-soluble dye. It will cause the wood to stain unevenly. It is only for oil-based stains.

To get even coloration, apply the stain liberally to the raw wood.

With a rag or paper towel, wipe off all the stain before it dries.

You can control the color of a pigmented stain by wiping off more or less, as you choose.

finished for contrast (see the photo at left). Make sure you leave plenty of drying time, at least overnight, so the thicker areas of stain dry completely before you seal them.

Specialty Stains

Mail-order catalogs and specialized wood-working stores carry a range of stains that give you far more control over coloring wood. These materials include ready-to-use stains that are clearly marked as either all dye or all pigment, chemical stains, and the raw ingredients you'll need to make your own stains, glazes, and tints. Dyes color wood differently than pigments, and having control over each separate coloring operation can be very handy. Some of these techniques are a challenge, but they open up many coloring options.

"Popping" the Grain

Figured wood has beautiful grain patterns that make it prized for woodworking. There are two simple ways to make the figure "pop" out with depth and shimmer. The simplest way is to coat the wood with oil. This creates a subtle, but deep color change and seals the wood at the same time. The downside is that it is not practical to dye the wood once it is sealed with oil. If you want to color the wood, and still want to "pop" the grain, do it with the two-step staining process described below.

For oil applications, liberally coat the wood with boiled linseed oil or Danish oil. Let the oil sit on the wood for at least 20 minutes, and then wipe off any excess with a clean rag or paper towel. Let the oil dry overnight before you proceed with your clear finish. (And remember to take care with the oily rags because they can ignite by themselves. Lay the rags or towels out one layer thick on a clothesline or on the edge of a table or trash can. When they are dry and hard, usually overnight, you can put them in the trash.)

If you prefer to "pop" and then dye the wood, stain the wood with a very dilute black or dark brown water-soluble dye

Boiled linseed oil brings out the figure of maple without adding too much color.

stain. A more intense dye will pop with more contrast but also add more dark color to the curls. With a nylon abrasive pad and water, scrub off as much of the dye as you can. Let the wood dry and lightly sand with 220 grit (see the top photo at right). You will find that the highlights will lighten, but the dark dye will not come out of the curls completely. Now restain with another dye for the color you want (see the bottom photo at right). The small amount of dark dye that remained in the figure makes it stand out.

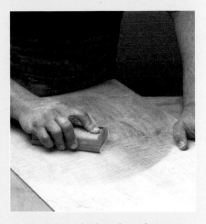

A weak but dark-colored "pre-stain" adds contrast to the grain, making it pop out through the color stain. After the first dye dries, sand the wood lightly.

Restain the area with your preferred color. Here an amber dye goes over prestained and sanded wood. The combination brings out the fine figure in this maple.

How do I ebonize a small maple box? I tried to dye it with black dye, and it came out a sort of bluish purple. Is there some secret to ebonizing?

Black dye is actually very dark blue or green, and unless you have a wood that will absorb a lot of it, it won't go completely black. You can help the dye along by adding more of it to the finish itself, and after several layers, you'll have a black finish.

To stain wood completely black, India ink is the best choice. India ink is actually a very finely ground pigment, so it will color completely and not give you the washed-out blues and greens that you'll get from dye. India ink comes in both oil-based and waterborne versions. Both versions work, but I generally prefer to use waterborne as a stain directly from the bottle without diluting it. Once it is dry, it will work under any finish.

Dye

Dyes are sold as powders and liquid concentrates that you can use to create stains, and also as ready-to-use dye stains. Dye powders come ready to dissolve into a specific solvent. Water-soluble dyes mix with water, alcohol-soluble dyes go into alcohol, and oil-soluble dyes dissolve in any oil-based solvent, such as mineral spirits, naphtha, or lacquer thinner. Start with an ounce of dye powder per pint of liquid and thin the mixture to get the intensity you want. Once the dyes are in liquid form, you can intermix them to make any color imaginable.

Of the three types of dye, water-soluble dyes are usually the most lightfast (they fade the least in sunlight) and stain deepest into wood. They are the easiest to apply and will color evenly without creat-

Dye concentrates are an easy way to make your own bright, fade-resistant dye stains. They mix instantly, so you can add them a little at a time into the appropriate solvent until the stain is dark enough to suit your needs.

ing lap marks, those overlapping lines caused by restaining an area that was already stained. They are compatible under virtually any finish, though they can bleed up into waterborne coatings. For dyeing raw wood, they are always my first choice.

Alcohol-soluble dyes dry the fastest. In fact, they dry so fast that most people spray them on to get even coverage. They are perfect for tinting shellac, which is also alcohol soluble. Alcohol dyes do not raise the grain of the wood as much as water, but they do raise it slightly.

Oil-soluble dyes fade the fastest and don't usually color as deeply. Once they are dissolved in lacquer thinner, you can use them to tint lacquer. They will not raise the grain of wood at all, so in cases where that is important, these dyes are the best choice.

Dye concentrates are premixed dyes in liquid form. They are quite concentrated and can be added to many different solvents to make stains, or they can be used to tint a variety of finishes. Check the label or spec sheet to see what solvents they are compatible with and how to mix them. Usually, the liquid concentrate will mix freely with most types of solvents, including water, alcohol, and lacquer thinner. Once you have thinned out the concentrate, it is the same as a ready-to-use liquid dye. Concentrates allow you to make very dark or richly colored dye stains, and they are convenient to store since just a few ounces of concentrate can make several gallons of stain.

Using dye takes no particular skill, partly because you control the color by how you mix it, not by how you apply it.

Flood the surface of the wood liberally with dye stain.

Wipe off all the excess dye stain before it dries.

Dyes should be brushed, sprayed, or wiped on liberally, then wiped off while they are still wet (see the photos at left). Leave on only what gets absorbed into the wood, and the stain will be uniform and even. Leaving excess dye to dry on the surface can cause your finish to peel off (delaminate) in the future. Since dyes do not seal the wood, you can reapply a second or third color of dye right on the wood. Each subsequent color alters the original, often making it lighter, but does not replace it entirely. Ultimately, you will end up with a combination of the colors you applied (see the photos on the facing page).

Tinting with dye In addition to staining raw wood with dye, you can add dyes to finishes to make tinted finishes. A tinted finish is simply one that has color added to the finish itself. Tinted varnish, often called staining varnish, is available in stores, but it is just as easy to make your own. With the right dye, you can tint any finish you want to use—shellac, lacquer, or even waterborne coatings. Dyes are the best choice for tinting finishes since they add color without completely obscuring the wood. (If you add pigment to a finish, you are in essence creating paint.)

Mix the dye first into its appropriate solvent, then add the premixed liquid to the finish and stir. Use alcohol-soluble dye for shellac, oil-soluble dye for lacquer or

Each application of a different color dye will add a new color to the wood and remove some, but not all, of the previous color. In this series, brown dye is applied first.

A red dye alters the brown but does not eliminate it completely.

Finally, a yellow dye, added as a round spot, alters the red, brown, and red-brown combination. You can work with these dyes indefinitely to create and change any color you need right on the wood.

I bought "medium walnut" stain for an oak cabinet, and it came out way too red. I don't want to make it much darker, but I'd sure like to get rid of that red. Is there anything I can do?

The rules for "correcting" stained wood are the same as those for mixing stain. There are three color pairs that I use to correct stains without making them too dark. The pairs are: red and green, purple and yellow, and blue and orange. Green neutralizes red, and red neutralizes green, and so on. If a stain is too red, add a bit of green (and vice versa) and it will go to a neutral brown. The same works for the other pairs. You can either add the complement directly to the stain or as a second staining operation.

To help remember the pairs, I think of red and green as the "Christmas colors" and purple and yellow as "Easter colors." You're on your own for blue and orange.

Of course, the best course of action is always prevention. In the future, try stain on scraps of the same wood as your furniture first, then buy or mix the right color.

varnish, and water-soluble dye for water-borne coatings. Just be careful to apply your coats of tinted finish very evenly, or you could end up with areas that are lighter or darker.

Removing dye Now and then you may find that no matter how many times you add a different dye to the wood, you still can't get the color you want. At that point you will wish you had a large dye "eraser" that would let you get back to the color of the raw wood and start all over again. You are in luck. Common household laundry bleach, applied full strength, will remove the dye but will not change the color of the wood (see the bottom photo at left). Use fresh bleach, sponge it on liberally, and let it dry overnight. By morning you will be ready to start anew. Brush off or sand off any of the white salt residue left on the surface and start over.

Pigment

Pigments are sold as powders, concentrates, and ready-to-use stains. Dry powders are convenient to use during touchup, but it is very difficult to mix them evenly into liquids for stains. To make things easier, I mix stains using pigments that are already in a liquid.

There are a few ready-to-use all-pigment stains available in the local hardware or home store. The problem is that they do not necessarily say so on the label. If you do find them, and you can't find

You can make a translucent-colored finish by adding alcohol-soluble dye to shellac or oil-soluble dye to lacquer or varnish.

You can completely remove a dye from unsealed wood by wiping it down with full-strength laundry bleach.

exactly the right color, you can intermix them to create a custom color.

You can also buy pigments in three highly concentrated forms: artist's oil colors, Japan colors, and UTCs (universal tinting colors). These are mixtures in which enough dry powdered pigment was mixed into a liquid base that they end up as a paste or very thick liquid. Artist's oils are pigments mixed into oil, usually linseed oil. Japan colors are artist's oils with Japan drier added to them in order to make them dry faster. UTCs are pigments added to a liquid that is compatible with most any finishing medium. You can use any of the three types of pigment pastes to alter the color of the oil-based stains you find in the store. Just be aware

I stained a solid-wood frame-and-panel door with a pigment stain. It looks good except where the stain went into the end grain that shows on the ends of the panel and ends of the frame. Those areas are way too dark. Any way to avoid this?

Pigments color by lodging in pores, nooks, and crannies. End grain has more and larger pores, so it grabs more pigment. There are two ways to prevent this, but no way to reverse it after you've stained.

You could try dye stains, which absorb into the wood and tend to color both flat and end grain more uniformly. However, they will not highlight the large grain patterns in woods like oak and ash as well as pigment stains will.

To get pigments to stain more uniformly, you must pre-seal all exposed end grain. Brush the end grain with a thin coat of glue size (watered-down glue) or a coat of dewaxed shellac before you stain.

Art supply stores and woodworking specialty stores carry artist's oils (right) and Japan colors (in cans at left). Universal tinting colors (the tubes in front of the cans at left) are sold in home stores, craft stores, and paint stores.

that by adding more color concentrate you may change the drying time.

Mixing your own pigment stain If you are so inclined, it is fairly easy to make pigment stain from scratch. You'll need at least one type of pigment paste, boiled linseed oil, and some thinner (see the top photo on the facing page). Start with equal amounts of oil and pigment paste and add as much thinner as you need to make it thin enough to control and flow easily. Try the stain on a scrap and then modify it. More pigment makes the stain richer in color, more oil makes it dry slower, and more thinner makes it lighter and faster drying.

Deep, Rich Mahogany

Old mahogany furniture often shows a depth and character that is hard to copy with simple staining. In fact, new mahogany is often fairly plain, and staining it only changes the color. Here's a way to create a rich cordovan mahogany that shimmers with deep golden highlights.

Stain the raw mahogany with a yellow-amber water-soluble dye. It will make the wood look too yellow, but don't worry, this is only the first step. When the dye is dry, restain the wood with a reddish-brown pigmented oil stain. Let it dry overnight, then seal the wood with a thin coat of dewaxed shellac.

Fill the pores with a dark reddish-brown pore filler. Let the filler dry completely (usually three days) and seal it with another coat of dewaxed shellac.

Brush or spray on a coat of lacquer or varnish. Now glaze the wood with asphaltum (roofing tar) mixed with mineral spirits and a dollop of linseed oil. Once the glaze is dry, proceed with several clear topcoats. When the finish is full and flat with no pores showing, buff it to high gloss.

It takes many layers of color to get a deep, rich brown mahogany with golden highlights, but the end result is impressive. From left to right, this panel shows the successive applications starting with raw mahogany, a yellow dye stain, a reddish-brown pigmented stain, dark cordovan pore filler, and finally asphaltum glaze.

Would you like a way to make it even easier? If you look at the ingredients in a can of paint, you will notice that it contains the same things that I told you to put into stain—pigment, oil, and thinner. In other words, pigment stain is simply thinned-out paint (whether oil based or latex). If you don't feel comfortable mixing colors, or don't want to assemble the ingredients, you can always buy a can of the right color paint and thin it down into a stain.

Applying pigment stain The easiest way to apply pigment stain is to flood it onto the wood and wipe it off before it dries. This works great on fairly porous woods like mahogany, poplar, or oak. You can also put the stain on heavier, and instead of wiping it all off, wipe off only

You can mix your own pigment stain or glaze with some pigment paste, like the Japan colors in the cans, a touch of boiled linseed oil, and some thinner.

You can make a quick and easy pigment stain by adding solvent to paint. Here the author has added water to a custom-color latex paint to make a waterborne pigment stain.

Pigment stain on top of dye gives you full control over the colors in the wood. A brown pigment stain (bottom of board) was applied over an amber dye (right side of board). The patch at the lower right shows how the two work together to look different than either stain alone.

as much as you want until you get the color you seek.

One of my favorite techniques for ash or oak is to apply a pigment stain over a dye stain. The dye goes on first and uniformly colors the wood. Once it is dry, I follow up with a pigmented stain and wipe it all off so that it only stays in the large "cathedral" pore patterns in the wood. This lets me control both the background color and the pore-pattern color in the wood.

Glazing Previously I showed you how to mix pigmented stain. Well, now you know how to mix glaze, because it is the same thing. In fact, the only difference between pigmented stain and glaze is where you put it. Stain goes on raw wood, and glaze goes between coats of finish. Of course, if you are not so inclined, there are pre-mixed ready-to-use glazes on the market. They will handle about the same as the ones you mix yourself.

Glazing can add the appearance of more depth to furniture with high and

FINISHING TALES

Trade Secrets

It was early in the 1970s when I bluffed my way into a job at a good-sized finishing shop in south Florida. I landed the job by convincing the owner that I knew everything about finishing. At the time, I probably believed that myself. No matter, within a few days we both knew the truth.

The shop had a secret finish called Golden Oak, and it was popular enough that we had developed a local reputation for it. We'd stain oak with a pigmented French ochre wiping stain on the raw wood, then seal it with a coat or two of lacquer. When that was dry, we'd glaze the wood with "special glaze," a dark, thick, oily concoction that was secured in the front office in unmarked cans.

One day the boss, Wade, called me into the office to reveal the secret formula for our special glaze. I was elated. Here was my chance to learn one of the coveted trade secrets that separate professional finishers from amateurs.

The "special glaze" was asphaltum (roofing tar), purchased from a local contractor and cut with mineral spirits to a liquid consistency. It was easy to understand the secrecy. Our high-class customers would be less than ecstatic to learn their oak antiques were being smeared with tar, even though the end result was rather alluring.

A few years later, I found myself working in one of the top finishing houses in New York. My first day on the job, I was checking out the familiar cans of finish on the shelf when, to my shock, I came across one labeled "asphaltum," and sure enough, it contained the old familiar glaze. Clearly, some cad had stolen Wade's secret formula and brought it up North. I quizzed one of the older employees about the can, and he looked at me as if I had just fallen off the turnip truck. It seems that asphaltum was a staple in every New York finishing shop, not only for glazing a variety of finishes but as a raw-wood stain as well. The local finishing-supply company had been selling asphaltum to shops for longer than my former boss had been alive. I smelled a rat.

It didn't take too long to figure out that Wade, who had been only a mediocre finisher in the competitive arena of New York, must have found himself as a big fish in the smaller pond of the Deep South. He parlayed his knowledge of asphaltum, a common material that had not yet arrived on the local Florida scene, into a finish based on a trade secret. Such is the stuff of myth.

As for me, I would never again be conned out of sharing information. I learned early on that in finishing, there are no trade secrets.

---

low areas, such as raised-panel doors, turned legs, and carvings (see the top photo on p. 96). The dark glaze is left in corners and recesses to enhance the three-dimensional contrast.

To glaze, start by sealing the wood with a thin coat of whatever sealer you choose.

Let it dry, lightly scuff it if it is not smooth, and add another thin coat just to get a smooth surface. Flood the glaze on and wipe it off the high areas (see the bottom left photo on p. 96). You'll notice that since the wood is sealed, the glaze sits on top, allowing you to wipe it off completely.

Glazing can add depth and contrast by putting color in recessed areas.

Flood the glaze onto the sealed wood and wipe off the high areas.

Blend dark and light areas with a China bristle brush, leaving extra stain in the grooves and recesses.

Leave the dark glaze in the low areas to accent the lines of the piece. Use a brush to blend the stain transition from dark to light areas (see the bottom right photo on the facing page). I like a 2-in. China bristle brush for this blending, but any brush you are comfortable with will work. Wait overnight for the glaze to dry before you add any more clear topcoats.

Pickling Dark pigment on light wood is called glazing. White or pastel pigment on wood (dark or light) is called pickling. The technique is exactly the same; only the color is different. In short, pickling is simply glazing with white or pastel-colored glaze. As with other colored glazes, you can either make it yourself with light-colored pigment pastes or buy it ready-to-use at the store.

Dry brushing One of the most unique ways to apply pigments to wood is by dry brushing. Applied to unsealed wood, dry brushing is basically the opposite of glazing. While glazing deposits colored pigment in the low recesses of furniture, dry brushing adds colored pigment to sharp edges and raised areas by "dirtying" the raw wood with an almost-dry, but pigment-laden brush (see the top photo on p. 98).

To do this technique, mix a fairly thick pigment stain, about the consistency of

Dry brushing brings out both the grain patterns and sharp edges on this raised panel.

Load the brush with color by rubbing the tips of the bristles through the pigment mixture.

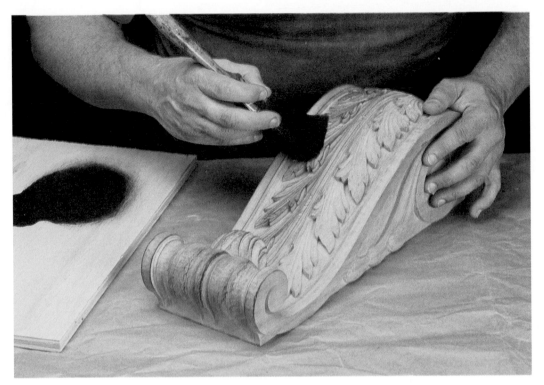

A light glancing stroke of the dirty bristles over the wood will deposit color onto the edges and raised areas of this carving.

A piece of sandpaper or nylon abrasive pad "erases" blotches caused by a brush that is too wet when dry brushing.

heavy cream, of just naphtha and Japan color. With a small brush, drop a dollop of the stain onto a smooth scrap board. Rub the tips of a good China bristle brush through the color until it looks dry on the board and on the brush, as shown in the bottom photo on p. 98. (If the brush is too wet, it will create blotches on the wood, which will have to be sanded out—see the bottom photo on p. 99.) Sweep the tips of the brush with light glancing strokes over the raised areas and sharp edges of raw, unsealed wood (see the top photo on p. 99). The brush should deposit a crisp or soft line of color, depending on how sharp the feature of the wood is. Dry-brushed color dries almost immediately, and you can seal the wood within the hour.

Chemical Stains

Any chemical that reacts with elements in the wood or with another chemical added to the wood is called a chemical stain. Many chemical stains are clear or a different color than the stain they create. Because they react with components in the wood, often the tannin, and because wood is not all the same, the results are often unpredictable. Most chemical stains are toxic or caustic and should be handled with great care, along with goggles, gloves, and a respirator. (For information on using chemical stains, see *Hand-Applied Finishes* by Jeff Jewitt, The Taunton Press, 1997.) If you are not familiar with handling dangerous chemicals, avoid them.

Recently, a safer alternative to chemical stains came on the market. Called Old Growth, it is a series of waterborne mixtures that are applied in two steps. These mixes approximate some of the effects that you can get with chemical stains without subjecting you to the danger. Some of the Old Growth formulas approximate the effects of traditional chemical stains, such as fumed oak, iron buff ebonizing, and aged cherry. They are distributed by Woodworker's Supply (800-645-9292). If the subject of chemical stains intrigues you, this is a good place to start.

Sealer, Primer, and Filler

The first coat of any clear finish that you put on raw wood acts as a sealer, because it dries to a film, however thin, that seals the wood. In other words, anything that dries to a film, even a thinned-out version of topcoat, becomes a sealer if you use it that way. Whether it is a coat of linseed oil, a brushful of varnish, or a spray coat of lacquer, it is by definition a sealer if it is the first coat you put on. Unfortunately, not all finishes do a good job of sealing raw wood, so coatings manufacturers have developed special sealers to help us out.

Not all woods or finishes require a sealer. In fact, some types of coatings, like oil varnish, are naturally self-sealing, and very dense woods, like rock maple and ebony, rarely benefit from a sealer at all. On the other hand, there are times when the right sealer can save lots of time and prevent finishing problems down the road. Sanding sealer, for example, can eliminate several coats of lacquer and make sanding easier when it's used on porous woods, like poplar or cherry.

While clear coatings are called sealers, solid-color pigmented sealers are known as primers. Not surprisingly, primer is used the same way as sealer, except that sealer goes under clear finishes while primer goes under solid-color finishes or paint. Filler, also called pore filler, is a different material altogether. It is a very thick mixture that can both seal wood and fill up pores at the same time, but it is normally used only to fill pores. Like sealer, filler is not always needed, but it can save loads of sanding time and result in better finishes. Filler is used to create pore-free, glass-smooth finishes over open-pore woods, like mahogany and walnut.

Sealer

Although any finish can theoretically act as a sealer, not all finish materials are equal when it comes to being "first coat." There are several different specialty sealers that deal with problems such as extremely porous woods or contaminated surfaces. But you don't always need one of these specialty sealers. Some finishes act as their own sealer. Oil, oil varnish, polyurethane, and shellac, for example, are self-sealing and usually do not require a sealer. In fact, shellac is so good as a sealer that it is fre-quently used under other finishes as a sealer instead of as a topcoat. Some fin-ishers like to thin the first coat of oil, varnish, or shellac with equal amounts of the appropriate thinner so that the sealer coat dries faster. However, these finishes will seal well no matter how you apply the first coat.

Some sealers exist just to save time. For example, the combination of a very porous wood, like poplar or pine, under brittle, hard-to-sand coatings, like lacquer, cries out for sanding sealer. Porous woods tend to suck up coats of lacquer like a

Sanding Sealer

Lacquer requires its own special sealer, called sanding sealer, and for a good rea-son. Lacquer is difficult to sand, and the first coats tend to be absorbed quickly into porous woods like pine, poplar, and lauan. Getting lacquer to stop disappear-ing into the wood and then sanding it smooth seems like an uphill battle. Sand-ing sealer seals the wood faster and is far easier to sand.

Sanding sealer is made by adding zinc stearate, a soft, fluffy material, to any lacquer—nitrocellulose, acrylic, or even waterborne. The sealer builds up faster than lacquer, so one or two coats of sand-ing sealer saves several coats of lacquer. The stearates make the finish very easy to sand and make it powder instead of getting gummy.

If you are using lacquer as a topcoat, start with sanding sealer, but no more than one or two coats. Lacquer, which is brittle, chips if it is sitting over a thick layer of soft sanding sealer, and the stearates in sanding sealer make it slightly milky.

Sanding sealer "powders" off and sands quickly and easily.

sponge absorbing water. A coat or two of soft sanding sealer will be easier to sand than hard lacquer and will plug up those thirsty pores faster, thus saving several coats of finish. Other sealers make different areas of wood take stain more uniformly. Glue size, used as a sealer, works well to make very porous end grain act like the flat grain nearby when the stain goes on (see the photo at right).

Sealer can also act as a barrier to prevent wax, oil, stain, or pitch from contaminating topcoats. Lacquer and waterborne coatings are particularly susceptible to these elements. A coat of dewaxed shellac, used as a sealer instead of a topcoat, stops contamination. As a bonus, it halts grain raising common to waterborne coatings. Sometimes the wood itself is the problem. Rosewood, for example, bleeds color into lacquer and contains chemicals that prevent oil varnish from curing. You can use both vinyl sealer and shellac to form a barrier that stops color from bleeding into lacquer and allows oil-based varnish to cure properly over rosewood. Finally, there are some finishes, such as two-part catalyzed lacquer or conversion varnish, that are designed to work hand-in-hand with a specially formulated sealer.

Below are some common sealers and the finishing problems they solve. With each problem I've paired the best sealer for the job. When in doubt, dewaxed shellac is the best all-around sealer.

Dewaxed shellac can be used as a sealer to solve most problems associated with

Unsealed end grain drinks up extra stain and finish (right). The left side of this panel's edge was sealed with glue size before being stained with a pigmented stain.

What sort of sealer is best to use under catalyzed lacquer? I've been told that it is not compatible with regular sanding sealer. Is that true?

Yes, it is true. In fact, catalyzed lacquer or conversion varnish requires a special sealer that is also catalyzed or reacted.

Most sealers are not particularly heat resistant. If you were to put a heat-sensitive sealer under catalyzed lacquer, which is very heat resistant, the sealer would be the weak link that ruined the heat resistance of the finish. Catalyzed lacquer or conversion varnish is generally sold along with its own special two-part sealer. Although you can use shellac or vinyl sealer under these coatings, it will make them somewhat less heat resistant.

Water-soluble dyes can "bleed" into waterborne finishes and may come off on your brush or rag. The dyed wood should be sealed first with dewaxed shellac.

I've been told shellac is the best sealer for coating furniture that has been stripped. I am about to refinish a table in polyurethane, and on the can it says "Do not use over shellac." Whom should I believe?

The polyurethane manufacturer does not fear the shellac itself, but rather the wax it often contains. Virtually all of the liquid shellac sold in cans contains wax. That is not unusual, since shellac in its natural state contains wax. (The one exception is the shellac in spray cans. The wax clogs up the tips, so they leave it out.) The problem is that finishes will not stick to wax. You will need to buy dewaxed shellac flakes and mix your own shellac.

Not all shellac sold in flakes is dewaxed, so you must specify that. The most common color of dewaxed flakes is super blonde, but it is also available in garnet. You'll probably notice that after it is mixed into a liquid, shellac with wax in it is cloudy, while dewaxed is clear. (For a guide to mixing shellac, see p. 125.)

waterborne finishes. A thin coat of dewaxed shellac will seal in water-soluble dye so it does not bleed (see the photo at left); it sticks well to oil stains, and waterborne coatings stick well to it; and it acts as an excellent barrier coat, sealing in any wax or oil to let the waterborne coating flow out as smoothly as it was designed to do. As an added bonus, dewaxed shellac prevents the grain raising caused by the water in the waterborne finish. Make the sealer by mixing 4 oz. of dewaxed shellac flakes into 1 pt. of denatured alcohol in a lidded glass or plastic jar. Stir or shake the mixture frequently, and it will be ready to use the next morning.

Dewaxed shellac also works on stripped furniture. After stripping, furniture often has stains, wax (from the stripper), and silicone or other oils (from polishes) in the wood. These contaminants can create drying and fisheye problems in the topcoat, especially lacquer (as shown in the photo on the facing page). You can avoid all these problems by sealing stripped pieces first with a thin coat or two of dewaxed shellac.

Vinyl sealer is the ideal solution for the problems associated with finishing wood in the *Dalbergia* family (rosewood, cocobolo, tulipwood). Oil-based varnish and polyurethane will not cure properly on these woods, and lacquer may cause the woods' natural colors to bleed into adjacent light-colored woods. Apply one coat of vinyl sealer and follow it with a coat of lacquer within 45 minutes in order to get good adhesion under a lacquer finish. The reason for the fast recoat time is that lacquer does not adhere well to cured vinyl sealer. In order to get it to stick, it is best to put lacquer on before the vinyl has a chance to cure.

After 45 minutes, the vinyl will be hard enough to recoat, but still soft enough for the lacquer to "bite" into it. If you must wait any longer, let the vinyl dry enough to sand and scuff-sand it with 320-grit paper before you move on to lacquer. This is not as much of a problem with varnish or polyurethane, which stick better to vinyl. For them, let the vinyl cure several hours and scuff-sand the vinyl before topcoating. You can buy vinyl sealer at stores that sell wood lacquer. If you can't find vinyl sealer, though, dewaxed shellac will also work.

Although not a finish, *glue size* can be used to seal the end grain of wood. End grain absorbs finish and stain more

Sealing with dewaxed shellac can prevent "fisheye" spots in waterborne and solvent-based lacquer. This lacquered walnut board clearly shows the craterlike fisheyes that result from contaminated wood.

Problems that Sealers Solve

Problem	Solution
Water-soluble dyes bleed up into waterborne finish.	Apply a thin coat of dewaxed shellac.
Waterborne coatings don't adhere over oil-based stain.	Apply a thin coat of dewaxed shellac.
Waterborne coatings and lacquer are very susceptible to any wax or oil contamination in the wood, especially on a piece that has been stripped.	Apply a thin coat of dewaxed shellac.
Members of the *Dalbergia* (rosewood) family can be difficult to finish.	Apply one coat of vinyl sealer (if you can't find vinyl sealer you can substitute dewaxed shellac).
End grain absorbs more finish.	Use glue size prior to finishing.

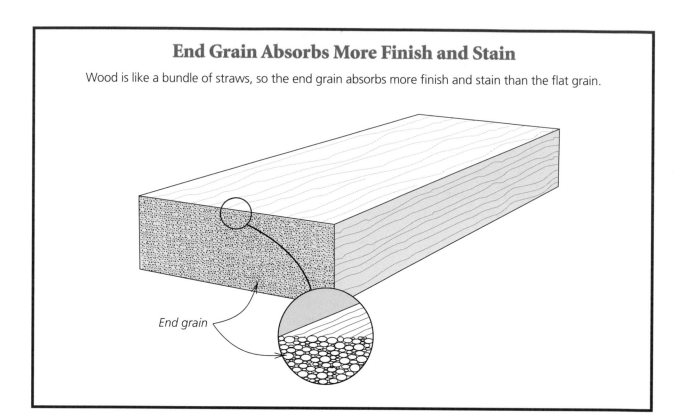

End Grain Absorbs More Finish and Stain

Wood is like a bundle of straws, so the end grain absorbs more finish and stain than the flat grain.

End grain

I'll be spraying a small side table in rust-colored lacquer. Should I seal the wood first with sealer, white undercoat, or primer?

The confusion comes from the terminology. Primer is simply colored sealer, and white undercoat is another name for primer. Since you are using a colored lacquer, I would use a white primer. You could use a clear sealer if you prefer, but the white primer will make it easier to see, and fix, any small dings or scratches in the surface. Even tiny marks will show up better when the wood is sprayed all one color, and it is better to find them during the primer coat than after the color is on.

than the adjacent flat grain (see the drawing above), but sealing it with glue size makes it act more like the rest of the wood (see the photo on p. 103). Glue size is sold commercially, but you can make your own by mixing white glue or hide glue 50/50 with water.

Primer

In woodworking, primer simply means sealer that is pigmented, usually white. It is frequently called "white undercoat" and, like sanding sealer, it builds fast and sands easily. Primer is used under colored lacquer or varnish to hide the variations in wood color and to make it easy to see if the surface is smooth enough for colored

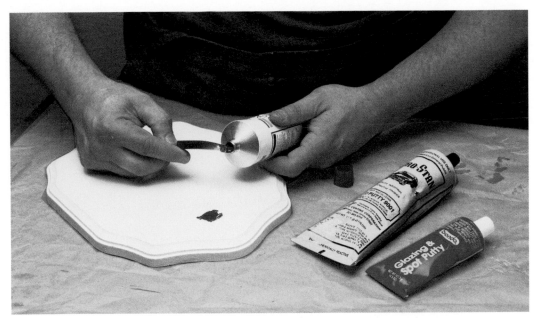

There are several brands of red spot putty, a fast-drying putty designed for filling small defects. It is sold in toothpaste-type tubes at auto stores and at some home stores.

topcoat. Every little defect shows up in a solid-color surface, whether it is white or another color. Primer will let you find defects and fill them before it is too late.

Brush or spray primer onto raw wood and sand it until it is smooth. If you sand through to the wood, touch up the area with more primer or add another coat, but make sure the entire surface is primed before you move on to color. You can fill small defects with the red spot putty sold in automotive stores (see the photo above).

For those times when you need the power of shellac to stop dyes, oils, and waxes from bleeding up into a solid-color finish, there is a white shellac-based primer called Zinsser BIN (see the photo at right). It sands well, coats and seals everything you'll run across, and is available in most any hardware, paint, or home store.

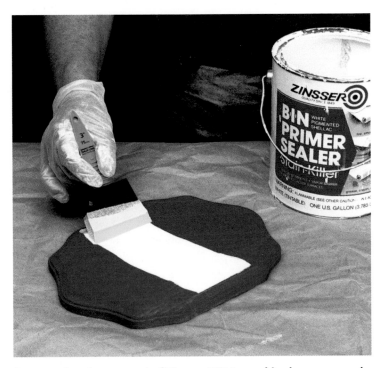

Spray or brush on a coat of Zinsser BIN to seal in dye, wax, and oil contamination under a solid-color finish. Here you can see how an application of BIN easily hides the red dye on this stained plaque.

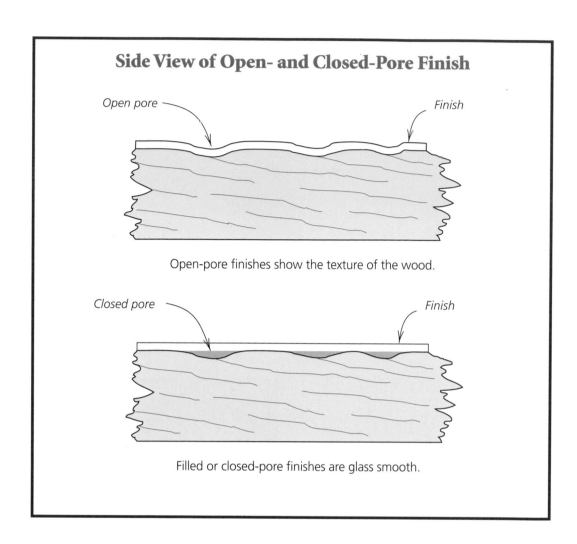

Side View of Open- and Closed-Pore Finish

Open pore

Finish

Open-pore finishes show the texture of the wood.

Closed pore

Finish

Filled or closed-pore finishes are glass smooth.

Which Comes First, the Filler or the Stain?

Pore filler usually contains colored pigment and, to a certain degree, will act like stain. However, there are times when you'll want more color or a different color in the wood.

Put dye stains on the raw wood *before* you fill. I prefer to use water-soluble dyes. They color deeply, and if you happen to sand through them while leveling the pore filler, they are easy to fix. Simply restain with the same concentration of dye in water after the filler is sanded.

If you are going to use a pigmented stain (or one that contains a combination of pigment and dye), apply it *after* the filler is on. You can control the pigment stain to leave on as much or as little color as you like, and it will work whether or not you have sealed the wood before filling.

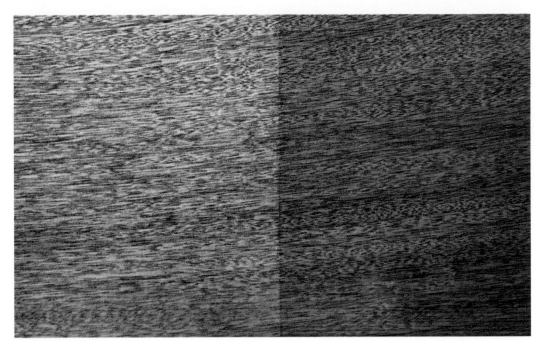

Pore Filler

Pore filler, sometimes called paste wood filler, is designed to fill the grain in open-pore woods, such as mahogany, walnut, rosewood, teak, and sometimes oak and ash. Filler is not always necessary. Most modern finishes allow the texture of wood to show. These are called open-pore finishes and do not require filler. Use filler only when you need a glassy, smooth finish with no pores showing. High-gloss finishes in particular look better with filled pores, though satin-sheen finishes look fine either way.

Pore filler is available as a fairly slow-drying oil-based mixture, as a faster-drying waterborne mixture, and as a clear waterborne filler. The first two look the same once they are dry, but each works best with a different application method.

Oil-Based Filler

Oil-based filler is a thick paste made of oil, solvent, and inert pigment (mostly ground quartz). It comes in a variety of colors and in "neutral" or "natural," which is not clear, but rather a pale ecru color. You can apply it directly to the raw wood or over wood that has been sealed with a thin coat of shellac. If you apply filler directly on the raw wood, it will color the wood as well as the pores, doing two jobs at once. If you apply it over sealed wood, it will color only the pores (see the photo above). Coloring just the pores gives you more contrast and more control of the appearance of the piece.

Oil-based filler comes in a variety of colors. You can buy the color you need, alter the color slightly, or start with neutral and make your own custom-color filler. Change the color by adding artist's

Use Japan colors to modify the color of oil-based filler. Remember that it will dry slightly lighter in color than it is wet.

I'm building a hutch using flat-cut ash and oak. This is my first time working with these woods, and I want a very natural-looking finish that shows off the character of the wood. A friend told me that because these are large-pore woods, I have to use pore filler first. Is that true?

No. You never have to use pore filler, and it is usually bypassed on ash and oak. The pores on ash and oak are quite large, and pore filler rarely makes them flat. To compound that, when these woods are flat cut, their grain forms dramatic "cathedral" pattern arches. As the wood dries, you can actually feel the undulation of the "hills" between the arched grain lines and the "valleys" around them.

Because finish is applied as a very thin film, it hugs these hills and valleys. Even if you were to fill the pores, you would still have this undulating effect. Most people feel that this defeats the purpose of pore filler, which is to create a glass-smooth surface. As a result, both ash and oak are generally left in an "open-pore" satin finish that needs no pore filler.

oils, UTCs (universal tinting colors), or Japan colors. Artist's oils will slow down the curing time of the filler, but UTCs and Japan colors will not. If you choose artist's oils, add an extra day or two of cure time before you sand.

Most filler comes as a thick, custard-like paste. To make it easier to handle, I thin it with mineral spirits to the consistency of heavy cream. The application process is the same whether you are working on raw wood or sealed wood, though you will notice that it is easier to remove filler from sealed wood. Use a brush or a piece of Scotch-Brite nylon abrasive pad to cover the surface with wet filler. Let the filler dry partially, but not too much. After about 10 minutes, the filler will start to turn hazy as it begins to dry. When this

FINISHING TALES

Three Men and a Table

Working with filler involves timing. You must catch the drying filler at just the right point or you won't have time to get the mud off before it hardens. If the mud comes off too soon, you will end up with partially filled pores. Let it sit too long and you inherit a disaster. Believe me, I know.

It was only my second day on a new job in a four-man finishing shop in New York City. The boss asked me to fill a mahogany conference table. I started brushing on the filler, and paused only when half the top was covered. I didn't want to coat more than

I could safely remove once it got cloudy, but I didn't want to look like I was just standing around doing nothing either. The filler still looked plenty wet, so I took a chance and covered the other half of the table.

When the whole top was coated I grabbed some burlap and started scrubbing off the now smoky filler. Within a minute I knew I was in trouble. The filler was drying much faster than I could get it off, and a huge expanse of conference table stretched out before me. I saw a vision of me spending

days trying to sand off the dried filler, followed by one of me looking for a new job.

Just as panic was setting in, I looked up to see the other three finishers surrounding the table, armed with burlap. In minutes, the four of us had all of the filler mud removed. The other three put down their burlap and went noiselessly back to their own benches. Not a single word had been spoken by anyone, and for all the time I worked in that shop, the incident was never mentioned. Nor was it ever forgotten.

happens, start packing the filler into the pores with a piece of burlap, then wipe off the excess filler with the burlap by rubbing across the grain. If you let the filler dry too long, you will not be able to get it off. If you wipe it off too soon, the pores will be only partially filled. Filler will not leave lap marks, so you can fill one section of the furniture at a time, wipe it off, and then move on to the adjacent section. Since set-up time is so important, start with a small section, about 2 ft. square, until you get some experience.

I like the look of filled pores, but I find paste wood pore filler messy and troublesome. Besides, it is opaque and I would rather see the wood itself. Why can't I simply build up lots of coats of shellac or lacquer, then sand it back until the pores are filled?

You can, but the pores will show up again in just a few months. If you fill pores with layers of finish, the coating will be at least twice as thick inside the pores as it is elsewhere. The finish will continue to shrink for several months. Because the percentage of shrinkage is the same and only the thickness is different, the pores will drop below the level of the rest of the finish and will show once again.

Applying Oil-Based Filler

Oil-based pore filler comes as a thick paste designed to level the pores in wood. You can apply it either to raw wood or to wood that has been sealed—the process is the same. To make the filler easier to handle, I like to thin it to the consistency of heavy cream by adding mineral spirits.

1 Brush filler on in any direction. It will look wet and glossy at first. Let it sit until it looks like hazy mud.

2 Pack the filler into the pores with a piece of burlap or jute.

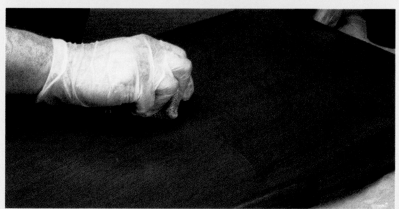

3 As the filler starts to dry, wipe it off across the grain with a fresh piece of burlap, jute, excelsior, or an abrasive-free nylon pad. Don't wipe too aggressively, or you will pull the filler back out of the pores. It's okay to leave it a bit dirty with the filler slightly "proud" in the pores, since your next step will be sanding.

When the filler is dry, sand off the excess with 320-grit paper, At first the paper may clog with random shiny spots.

The spots will soon be replaced with a regular dust pattern.

Once the filler is removed, let it dry completely. I always allow three days for oil-based filler to dry. Sealing filler that is not yet dry can cause the pores to turn gray under the finish several months later.

When the filler is dry, there will be a slight haze of filler on the surface in between the pores. Sand the surface with 320-grit self-lubricating sandpaper to remove this haze and to level the filler in the pores (see the photos above).

If you used a water-soluble dye and cut through the stain in spots, now is the time to restain with the same concentration of dye (see the top photo on p. 114). Restaining with the same dye will not change the color, but it will blend in any areas that were sanded through. You can also apply a pigmented stain at this point (see the bottom photo on p. 114). Once the stain or dye is dry, reseal the wood

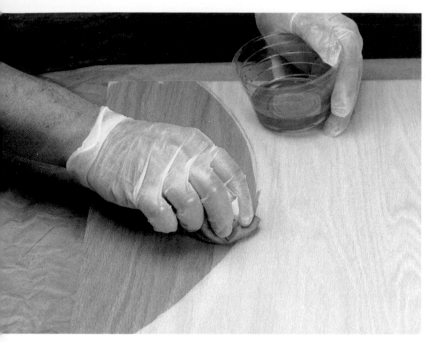

Stain the wood both before and after filling with the same water-soluble dye to correct any areas that were sanded through. Water-soluble dyes recolor only those areas that were sanded through and leave you with a uniform color.

Pigmented stain, like this light reddish stain, should go on after the pore filler.

and filler with a thin coat of dewaxed shellac before you move on to your chosen topcoat.

Waterborne Filler

Like its oil-based counterpart, waterborne filler is a thick paste of inert pigment. It contains a mixture of pigments, acrylic resin, water, and compatible solvents. The filler is usually thin enough to use from the can, but you can add water if you like. The major difference is that it cures much faster than oil-based filler and can be ready to recoat in less than a day. Waterborne filler comes in colors and in neutral ecru. To change the color, use UTCs.

Brush the filler on, and start to pack it into the pores with burlap. There is no need to wait until it gets hazy; it will quickly thicken while you are working. Once it is packed and starts to dry, squeegee it off with a credit card or any flexible plastic scraper (see the photos on the facing page). Waterborne filler will be dry enough to sand by the next morning. Sand, stain, and seal the same as you would with oil-based filler, and you are ready for the next coat of finish.

Clear Filler

There may be times when you want filled pores but don't want an opaque-colored filler. The latest entry in the field is clear waterborne fillers. They act a lot like the other waterborne paste wood fillers, but they dry clear.

Oil *Based* but Water*borne*?

You may have noticed that throughout this book I use the term *oil based* for oil finishes, colors, and fillers, but when it comes to water, I use the term *waterborne,* or in the case of dyes, *water soluble*. This is not a hard-and-fast rule. In fact, you'll frequently find other writers and manufacturers using the term *water based*.

Technically speaking, oil varnish, polyurethane, stain, and fillers are based on oil. The oil is the binder that remains behind after the solvent evaporates.

However, water is not a binder, and in finishes, dyes, and fillers that contain it, the water evaporates. In other words, the material is carried (borne) by water but is not really based on it.

Why not use water soluble? Because these materials are not soluble in water. Dyes are, but they are the exception. Waterborne coatings are impervious to water once they dry. If they were water soluble, they would melt when you cleaned them with a damp sponge.

A credit card is perfect for removing excess waterborne wood filler.

Old credit cards can be cut to various profiles for removing filler on moldings.

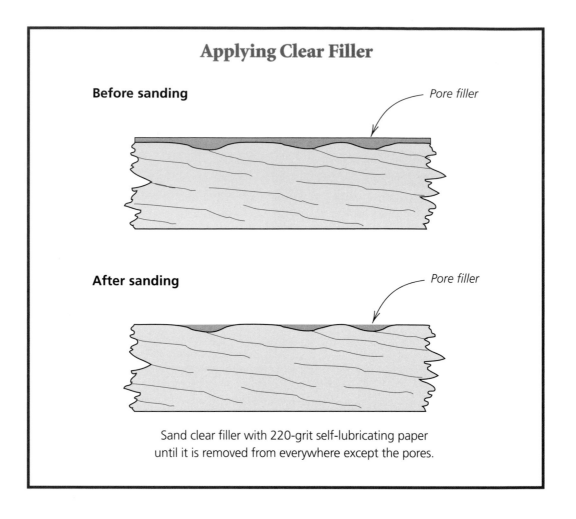

Applying Clear Filler

Before sanding

Pore filler

After sanding

Pore filler

Sand clear filler with 220-grit self-lubricating paper until it is removed from everywhere except the pores.

Clear filler is a thick, mayonnaise-like material that is compatible under most finishes. Clear filler works best if you trowel it onto the raw wood with a plastic putty knife or scraper and squeegee it off immediately. It may be slightly milky at first, but it will dry clear in just a few hours. The filler shrinks as it dries, so you might need a second coat. Let it dry overnight, then sand until there is filler only in the pores and none on the surrounding surface.

The major difference between this clear filler and other waterborne fillers is the way you color the wood. This is the one time you can stain last, since the filler itself will accept both water- and solvent-soluble dye stain as well as pigmented stain. After staining, seal with a coat of dewaxed shellac and move on to your finish.

Applying the Finish

By now you probably feel as if you've done it all. You have chosen the finish and applicators; stripped, sanded, puttied, stained, and sealed; and, at long last, are ready for the big event—the topcoat. If everything up until now was preparation, applying the topcoat is surely the main event.

But before you open the first can of finish, you have a couple of important decisions to make. The first is where to do your finishing. In some ways finishing is a delicate operation, and it makes sense to work in an area that is both safe and comfortable for you and the finish. Just like you, finishes need a clean area with just the right temperature and humidity for them to perform best.

Oddly enough, you also have to decide when to apply finish, and it is not always after the piece is glued up and sanded. Prefinishing, which means finishing all or some of the parts before you assemble them, is often far more convenient than waiting until all the woodworking is done.

Once those decisions are made it's time to figure out which of the many ways to apply a finish you should choose. I'll give you guidelines on what to use and how to do it. We'll cover everything from rags to brushes to spray guns, how to avoid problems, and which method goes best with each type of finish.

Where to Finish

Finishes are affected by dust, temperature, and humidity, and no matter how they are applied, they give off solvent fumes.

Apply finishes in a well-lit, dust-free room with good ventilation. Try to keep the temperature around 70°F and the relative humidity (RH) around 45%.

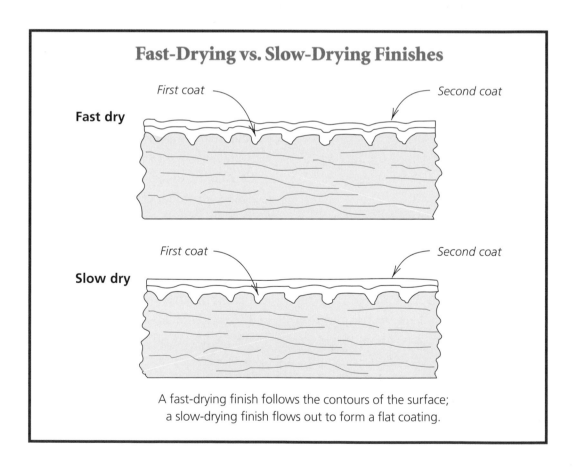

Fast-Drying vs. Slow-Drying Finishes

Fast dry

First coat — Second coat

Slow dry

First coat — Second coat

A fast-drying finish follows the contours of the surface;
a slow-drying finish flows out to form a flat coating.

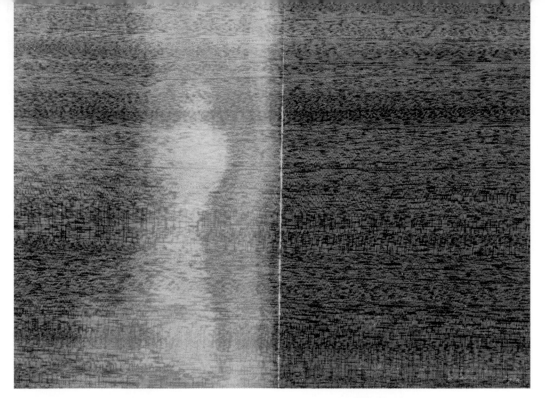

Very high humidity, above 85% RH, can cause a white haze called blush in lacquer (above, left side of board). It can also slow down the cure time of oil varnish and polyurethane and prevent waterbornes from curing. Wait for a drier day to do your finishing.

The ideal finishing area is a dust-free, well-lit, and well-ventilated room with a temperature around 70°F and a relative humidity of about 45%.

Solvent-based finishes dry and cure faster in warmer temperatures. However, they have more time to flow out and level in cooler temperatures. More leveling time means fewer brush marks but can also mean more sags and runs. It would be ideal to apply fast-drying finishes, like shellac and lacquer, in the cool of the evening when the temperature is around 60°F, and slow-drying finishes, like oil-based varnish and polyurethane, on a hot, dry 80°F day. Very high temperatures

(above 95°F) may cause pinholes and air bubbles in some lacquers, while very low temperatures (below 55°F) prevent many finishes from curing. It is best to avoid finishing when the temperature is below 60°F or above 90°F.

High humidity makes varnish dry slower and can cause lacquer to blush (see the photo above). Waterborne coatings may not cure properly if the relative humidity is over 85%. They will appear to dry but will flake off when touched. Low humidity is not a problem, but put off finishing if the humidity is too high.

Finish First, then Assemble

1 Start by sanding all the parts until they are ready to finish. Assemble the piece dry with no glue and mark the glue joints lightly in pencil.

2 Dismantle the piece and tape off the glue joint with 2090 Long Mask tape about 1/16 in. inside the pencil line. Erase the line before you stain.

3 Seal, finish, rub, or even wax the finish before you glue up the parts. Remove the tape by pulling it back over itself and about 30° away from the finish line.

Stain and seal floating or fixed panels first with just one coat of sealer. After glue-up, stain and seal the frame, and then topcoat the entire piece together.

A mist of overspray will get trapped inside the walls of this cabinet. It is likely to dry on the wood, leaving it rough as sandpaper. Prefinishing would prevent the problem.

Last week I started finishing an oak cabinet with Danish oil. It went on easily and looked great. I followed the directions, flooding it on and wiping it off 15 minutes later. However, when I came back the next day, it was as rough as sandpaper. When I looked closely, there were tiny bumps of dried finish at each of the large pores in the oak. What do I do now?

Now that it is dry, sand lightly with 320-grit self-lubricating paper to remove the bumps, then apply another coat of Danish oil.

Danish oil has a tendency to "creep" back out of the grain in large-pore woods, like oak and ash, drying to the "bumps" you described. This problem does not show up in smaller-pore woods. You can deal with it by wiping the piece repeatedly every hour or so until it dries, which is very labor intensive, or by letting it go (as you did) and sanding the next day. Other options include sanding the Danish oil into the wood. By sanding the oil into the surface with 400- or 600-grit paper, you create a thick slurry that is less likely to creep back out. Finally, you could choose one of the thick gel wipe-on finishes instead when you are faced with large-pore woods.

When to Finish

Many of us assume that applying finish is the last step in building furniture, done only after all the assembly is complete. However, it is usually possible to finish some or all of the parts before they are assembled. Prefinishing, as it is called, generally results in a far better and easier finishing job. Almost all case goods, many chairs, cabinets, and even boxes can be completely or partially prefinished.

Prefinishing prevents glue spots under the stain, because the stain goes on before the glue and virtually eliminates runs and sags by allowing you to coat all pieces horizontally. Even sprayed pieces come out better when there are no inside corners to catch overspray that bounces back from the wood and settles on the freshly coated pieces. When it is time to assemble the furniture, any glue squeeze-out easily wipes off the finished surface, and dried glue pops off with the aid of a sharpened dowel.

FINISHING TALES

Tradition

The first time David called me it was to ask about an authentic, hand-rubbed oil finish. In my own defense, I must say that I did everything I could to talk him out of it, but he was an adamant traditionalist. I was certain that if I described the process to him, he would think I was pulling his leg, so I took him to meet Tony.

An old-world finisher and former teacher of mine, Tony had already passed retirement age at a gallop, but he was still keeping shop hours in a cramped and cluttered New York walkup. The dusty old sample he showed us looked nothing like the one-coat wipes that pass for oiled walnut today. It was deep and rich and glossy, and I knew immediately that any hope of discouraging David was now lost.

In his heavy Italian accent, Tony described the arduous process. Start by sanding until the wood is perfectly smooth, he told us, then sand some more. When you are sure there are no scratches left with 220-grit paper, start adding linseed oil and sand with finer wet/dry paper. He explained how sanding the linseed oil into the wood with 400-, then 600-grit paper would create a

slurry of the oil and wood dust that would leave the surface smooth and start to fill the pores.

Finally, Tony came to "the rule of two," and I was sure this would be the clincher. "Use your bare hand," he said, showing us a leathery, calloused palm, "and rub oil into the tabletop 'til you can't stand the heat no more. Rub it twice a day for a week, twice a week for a month, twice a month for a year, and twice a year for life. Keep after it, and it will always be beautiful."
"That's not a finish," remarked David after we left the shop, "it's perpetual maintenance."

So when David called a second time for a traditional recipe, I was delighted he had chosen something simpler. He had heard of a home-brew mixture of beeswax, linseed oil, and turpentine and was hot to try it. I made it clear that this was not a durable bar-top finish; it is the sort of thing you use to wipe down exposed ceiling beams or other woodwork that needs to look good but takes no wear.

I also warned him of the smell. I told him to start by melting the wax, then mix in equal parts (1:1:1) of linseed oil and

turpentine while the wax was still liquid. Finally, I described how to wipe it on with burlap while it was still warm. At the time, it didn't occur to me to suggest a double boiler to heat the wax mixture.

Apparently, it didn't occur to him either. When I visited his shop a week later, my reception was on the chilly side. It was easy to see why. On his bench stood a one-burner hot plate supporting a rather blackened kitchen pot. Directly above on the otherwise white drywall ceiling was a sooty stain about the size of a deflated basketball indicating the spot where flames had recently danced toward the ceiling. "Did I mention anything about a double boiler?" I asked in my most innocent voice. David just glowered.

Shortly after that, I noticed that David had developed a curious fondness for modern, ready-mixed finishes and an equally curious aversion to soliciting my advice.

For a smoother oil finish on unstained wood, sand the first coat into the wood with 400-grit wet/dry paper. The oil and sawdust slurry will help fill the pores as well. Wipe off any excess slurry after 5 or 10 minutes.

Applying Finishes by Rag

A rag is the simplest tool you can use to apply a finish. It is quick, efficient, and the only method where you don't have to worry about dust settling on the surface. Oil, Danish oil, wax, gel varnish or polyurethane, wiping varnish, and shellac can all be applied with a rag.

For the most part, applying a finish with a rag is simply a matter of wiping it on, then wiping it off. This allows only a small amount of finish to stay on the wood. It has the advantage of avoiding application problems, like drips and runs, but it is a slow way to build up a thick finish. For each of the finishes that work well when applied by rag, I'll give you some guidelines on the best way to work with them.

French polishing, which uses a rag in the shape of a pad to apply finish, also falls in this category. However, it requires more skill and practice, and is specifically used to apply only one finish—shellac. The advantage is that the shellac remains dust free and drip free and can be built up fairly quickly to a thick, glossy coat with no equipment other than some cloth.

Oil or Danish Oil

Use a rag to flood the wood liberally with oil or Danish oil. Once the finish has sat for about 10 to 15 minutes, wipe off any excess that's on the surface. Let the finish dry overnight and repeat. Two or three coats give you an adequate finish, but building up more adds depth and gloss. You can apply oil or Danish oil similarly by flooding it on with a brush, then wiping with a clean rag.

If the varnish or gel looks streaky, wipe it with a clean cloth. You will still leave a reasonable amount on the wood.

To build up the finish a bit faster, and to get an exceptionally smooth surface, sand the first two coats into the wood. Use some fine 400-grit sandpaper to sand the wet oil into the wood (see the photo on p. 123). The sanding operation creates a slurry of sanding dust mixed with the oil that helps fill pores quicker. Sanding with the oil makes the surface smooth and silky. When you are finished sanding, wipe off any excess slurry on the surface. Use this technique only for unstained wood, since you are likely to cut through stain while sanding.

Wiping Varnish and Gel

The only difference between wiping varnish and gel and the oils is that you don't wipe them off as aggressively. They are generally thicker, so more of the finish tends to remain on the wood, even after wiping. For both wiping varnish and gel coatings, wipe them on, then rewipe

immediately with the same varnish-soaked cloth to even them out. Let each coat dry overnight. Because they are thicker, these coatings build a bit faster than the thinner oil mixtures. Two or three coats are usually quite enough, and at times you can get by with just one. If you like, you can make your own wiping varnish by adding a cup of boiled linseed oil to a quart of oil-based varnish or polyurethane.

Shellac

I like to flood on and wipe off a coat of thin dewaxed shellac as a sealer under lacquer, varnish, and even French polish, or as the first step of a brushed or sprayed shellac finish. I mix 4 oz. of shellac flakes in 1 pt. of denatured alcohol (see the sidebar on the facing page) and flood it liberally onto the wood, letting any end-grain areas drink up as much as they can. I flood on the shellac until it stops absorbing into the wood, then wipe off any excess with a

Mixing Shellac

It is quite easy to mix your own shellac, but you might wonder why you'd want to when you can buy it premixed. Shellac has a fairly short shelf life once it is mixed with alcohol. It starts to convert to softer shellac esters. As more shellac converts, the finish it forms takes longer to dry, is softer, and is more prone to water spotting. Most shellac sold in liquid form contains wax. The exception is shellac in spray cans, which is usually wax-free because the wax clogs the spray tips. Wax makes shellac easier to sand but also makes it less glossy and more susceptible to water spotting. Worse, most coatings will not adhere to wax, so shellac with wax in it is not appropriate as a sealer.

Shellac flakes, on the other hand, have a rather long shelf life if they are stored away from heat and sunlight. By buying shellac in flake form, you can mix only what you intend to use for a particular job. Shellac flakes are available through most wood-working mail-order specialty catalogs. You can buy flakes with wax or without (dewaxed) and in several colors from the lightest super blonde to dark garnet.

You can mix pretty much any amount of shellac in pretty much any amount of alcohol. After you mix it, you can thin it out by adding more alcohol. To make a good thickness for sealer or French polish, I mix 4 oz. of flakes to 1 pt. of denatured alcohol. Shaken frequently, it is ready to use by morning. Once shellac dries, it is the same whether you mix it thick or thin, but thinner shellac dries faster and is easier to brush.

In the inevitable case where you don't use all the shellac you mix, write a date on it and try to use it up within six months. If you're not sure if your liquid shellac is too old to use, put a drop on a piece of glass. It should be dry to the touch in 15 minutes. Let it dry overnight and scrape it with your fingernail. It should be brittle, not gummy. If the shellac fails either of these tests, throw it out and mix a new batch.

An easy way to mix shellac without measuring is to mark a jar with the amount of shellac you will need. Mark another line halfway to the first line. Fill to the lower line with flakes, then fill to the upper line with denatured alcohol. Shake it periodically until it is dissolved completely, usually overnight.

Recently I purchased an unfinished pine bread box and stained and finished it. I used oil-based polyurethane for the clear finish over a cherry stain. I have not been able to use the box because whenever we close the lid the stench of the polyurethane permeates into anything put into it. What can I do to eliminate the smell?

Your best bet is to lightly scuff-sand both inner and outer surfaces and seal them with several coats of shellac. As you have discovered, oil-based coatings add their distinctive odor to bread boxes and the inside of drawers. Shellac would have been a far better choice to start with, and even now will soon seal in most of the offending odor.

cloth dampened with alcohol. In about 20 minutes, the surface is dry and ready for the next coat of finish. Alcohol raises the grain of the wood, so sand very lightly with 320-grit self-lubricating paper before the next coat of finish.

French Polishing

Once you have sealed wood in shellac, you can continue to use a rag to build up a thicker finish. Rubbing shellac onto the wood with a pad is called French polishing. The friction and heat from rubbing in the finish make the shellac go on virtually dry, so there is no problem with dust settling on it. You can continue to build up the finish until it is thick enough or until you get tired. If the finish starts to get too soft or gummy, stop and let it dry, and come back to it later.

The problem with French polish is that the shellac-laden pad can either apply finish or take it off, depending on how you manipulate it. By gently squeezing the pad, you flow finish onto the surface. Keep the pad moving at all times and try to deposit an even amount of shellac on the entire surface. If you stop the pad while it is touching the surface, it will quickly melt the finish and leave an impression of the cloth in the finish. Think of the pad like an airplane that must be moving before you "touch down" onto the surface of the wood, and continue moving it until after you "take off."

For a more in-depth discussion of French Polishing, see *Hand-Applied Finishes* by Jeff Jewitt (The Taunton Press, 1997).

The French Polishing Pattern

Keep the pad in motion the entire time you polish, including when you touch down on the wood and lift off. Stopping the pad will result in a cloth mark in the finish. Rub the wet pad in circular or figure-8 patterns, covering the entire surface.

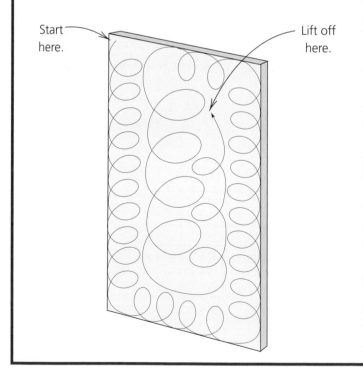

Start here.

Lift off here.

French Polishing

French polishing is a process with a long history and a reputation for being difficult and arcane, but it is really not that hard. Simply put, it means to apply a thin, even coat of shellac with a "pad" of cloth. This photo sequence will show you how to make a pad, load it with shellac and, if needed, mineral oil, and finish off the process at the end.

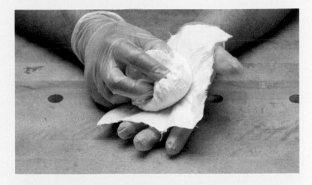

1 Take a golf-ball-sized wad of cheesecloth and wrap it tightly in a piece of linen.

2 Soak the pad in alcohol, wring it out, then "load" it with a squirt of thin shellac from a squeeze bottle.

3 The pad should be about as wet as a healthy dog's nose. Tamp the pad into the palm of your hand to test its wetness and to help distribute the shellac throughout the pad.

4 When the pad starts to dry out during application, recharge it with another squirt of shellac or alcohol. If the pad starts to stick, put a drop or two of mineral oil onto it. The mineral oil will rise to the surface when the shellac dries.

5 After the finish is dry, you can remove the mineral oil from the surface by lightly glancing over it in one direction with a clean pad slightly dampened with alcohol. This is called "clearing" or "spiriting off."

Applying Finishes by Brush or Paint Pad

Oil varnish and polyurethane, shellac, brushable lacquer, and waterborne coatings are all ideal candidates for brush or pad application. Brushes are very efficient, wasting little or no finish. They allow you to apply finish quickly to any shape or size piece, and they are easy to learn how to use.

For each of the finish groups described below, I've suggested both a type of brush or applicator and a method to apply the finish. However, these are guidelines, not rules. Use what works best for you. If you have a method that works well, stick with it; but if you are not sure, this is a good place to start.

Remember to always preload your brush with the appropriate solvent, and clean your brushes thoroughly once you are finished with them. You might want to take a few minutes to go back and re-read the section on caring for your brushes on pp. 29-31.

Oil-Based Varnish and Polyurethane

I prefer a natural China bristle or badger-hair brush for oil-based finishes. Choose one with a chisel end, long bristles, and flagged tips. (For more on choosing a brush, see pp. 26-29.) Soak the brush in mineral spirits all the way to the ferrule for about a minute, then squeeze out the excess, leaving the brush wet but not dripping.

Most varnish and polyurethane comes a bit too thick to brush easily. Stir the finish gently, then pour some out into a clean container. Thin it by stirring in about 1 oz. of mineral spirits or naphtha for each pint of varnish.

Whenever possible, lay the piece down so that you are coating a horizontal surface. Varnish flows out and dries slowly, so it's susceptible to sags and runs. When you can't prefinish or lay each side down, coat the piece upside down. If you do get sags, they won't be as visible once you turn the piece right side up again. If you see runs while the varnish is still wet, unload the brush and "pick up the run" by tipping off the area (see below).

Dip the brush only about one-third of the way into the varnish and touch the bristles to the side of the container to prevent drips (see the photos on p. 130). Hold the brush at a 45° angle and move the brush slowly, about 8 seconds per foot, with the grain, letting the varnish slide gently off the top of the bristles onto the wood. When you come to the end of a stroke, lift the brush while it's still moving forward so you don't flop the deflected bristles over the edge and create drips. Redip as needed. If the varnish starts to dry or get thick and sticky toward the top of the brush, stop and rinse the brush quickly in mineral spirits. Squeeze out the excess, redip the brush in varnish, and continue.

When you have finished brushing one surface, unload the brush by scraping it

Thinning Solvents

Type of finish	Fast solvent	Slow solvent (retarder)
Wax	Naphtha	Mineral spirits
All oil-based finishes (oil, Danish oil, varnish, polyurethane)	Naphtha	Mineral spirits
Shellac	Denatured alcohol	Butyl alcohol, small amounts of lacquer retarder (butyl cellosolve), Behlen's Behkol solvent
Lacquer	Lacquer thinner	Lacquer retarder (butyl cellosolve)
Conversion varnish, catalyzed lacquer	Special thinners sold with the coating	Special retarders sold with the coating
Waterborne coatings*	Distilled water (10% or less)	Lacquer retarder (butyl cellosolve)

Whether a waterborne thinner is fast or slow depends on the relative humidity. In dry air (low relative humidity), water will evaporate faster than butyl cellosolve. In wet air (high relative humidity), water will evaporate slower than butyl cellosolve.

Does it matter if I thin varnish with mineral spirits or naphtha? I know naphtha evaporates faster, but will that change the durability of the finish or only speed up its cure?

Actually, it will do neither. Changing the thinning solvent may speed up the tack time—the time it takes for the solvent to "flash off," or evaporate. However, the cure time has almost nothing to do with the speed of the solvent.

The finish cures by polymerization, a process that takes many hours. Although a slower solvent may prolong the start of the cure, it is really negligible. In any case, you end up with the same cured film no matter which thinning solvent you use. A slower solvent will give the coating more time to flow into pores and blend out brush marks but will also give it more time to sag on vertical surfaces.

Brushing Varnish

1 Dip only the lower third of the bristles into the varnish.

2 Touch the tips gently to the inside wall of the container to remove excess finish. Don't scrape the brush over the rim; that will unload it.

3 Hold the brush at about 45° and press down just enough to deflect the tip of the bristles. Move the brush slowly along the grain at about 8 seconds per foot.

4 Increase downward pressure on the brush without changing the angle as you get toward the end of the stroke. This feeds more finish to the tips.

5 At the end of the stroke, gently lift the brush while still moving forward.

6 Go back and tip off the surface by holding the brush at 90° to the surface. First unload the brush by scraping the bristles on the edge of the container. Then, brushing with the grain, run the tips of the bristles very lightly through the varnish.

across the edge of the container. Hold the brush at 90° to the wood and drag the tips of the bristles through the still-wet varnish to remove air bubbles and brush marks. This is called tipping off. On very large surfaces, stop and tip off after about 10 minutes of brushing. (To get a sense of the speed and style of good brushing technique, watch *The Woodfinishing Video with Michael Dresdner;* The Taunton Press, 1992.)

Shellac and Brushing Lacquer

Brushing lacquer is formulated to dry more slowly than spray lacquer, allowing more time for it to flow out and hide brush marks. Nevertheless, both shellac and brushing lacquer dry fast enough that they need a slightly different technique than the one you'd use for oil varnish. I like to use either a China bristle or fitch brush for both these materials.

Saturate the bristles in alcohol (for shellac) or lacquer thinner (for lacquer). Squeeze out the excess and dip one-third of the brush into the finish. Brush slowly in the direction of the grain (as in the photos on the facing page). At the end of each stroke, go back and tip off the stroke you just finished. Don't wait until you have brushed a large area, or the finish will be too dry to tip off. Once you have applied and tipped off the stroke, do not go back and rebrush it later. Shellac and brushing lacquer dry fast, so you only get one shot at getting it right. If you get a sag or run, unless you see it immediately,

leave it alone. Brushing it after the finish has started to set up will make it worse. (I'll show you how to fix sags and runs in the next chapter.)

It may seem as if the finish is setting up too fast and the brush marks will not flow out enough. You can help it along by brushing very thin coats. They will set up quickly but are less likely to result in offensive brush marks. You might also want to brush these finishes in cooler weather or in the evening, when the shop temperature drops down toward 60°F or 65°F. Cooler temperature will mean slower solvent evaporation, and the finish will have more time to flow out. You might also want to add a small amount of lacquer retarder (butyl cellosolve) to slow down the evaporation rate of the solvent. It will work for both lacquer and shellac.

Waterborne Coatings

Water causes natural bristles to splay when they get wet, so choose a nylon brush for waterborne coatings. For large, flat surfaces, paint pads work quite nicely. If you look carefully at the surface of the pad you will notice that it is covered with thousands of tiny bristles. Each is long enough to hold finish, but short enough so that the bristles don't cause excessive foaming. Long-bristle brushes often create a wealth of tiny air bubbles, called foam, by whipping through the wet finish. The large surface area of the pad combined with these short bristles yields an excellent tool for holding and spreading thin layers of waterborne coatings.

Using a Paint Pad

1 Load the pad by dipping the surface into the finish. Pouring some finish out into a flat-bottom pan makes it easier to control how you load the pad.

2 Gently scrape off the excess finish and let it run back into the pan. Waterborne coating should always be applied in thin coats.

3 After each stroke with the grain, go back and go over it once again to smooth it out. After that, move on and do not rework that area again.

Because waterborne coatings dry quite fast, the method for brushing them is about the same as for shellac and brushing lacquer—only the solvent is different. Soak the bristles in water and squeeze out the excess. Dip one-third of the brush (or the bristles on the pad) in the finish, touch off the tips, and begin the brush stroke. Whether you use a brush or a pad, go back and smooth out each stroke immediately, then move on and do not return to that swath.

Applying Finishes by Spray Gun

Spray guns take liquid finish and mix it with air to atomize it into small droplets. These droplets are propelled toward the wood at fairly high speed, allowing you to apply a thin coat evenly and quickly. Once the finish hits the wood, you want it to stay where you sprayed it and not run or sag. To make sure that happens, spray finishes like lacquer, shellac, conversion varnish, catalyzed lacquer, and waterborne coatings are formulated to dry very fast.

Spraying 101

Never sprayed before? Thinking of investing in a gun, compressor, and spray booth, and not sure it all suits you? Why not try spraying with an aerosol can first, and see how you like it. In fact, if you need to spray solid-color lacquer and you are not sure of your color-mixing abilities, spray cans are an easy way around that problem, too.

Spray cans of colored lacquer are sold under brand names such as Krylon in home, automotive, and hardware stores. They are very thin lacquer mixtures designed to be easy to spray. They come in a variety of colors and clear, as well as sealer, shellac, and even BIN primer sealer. Couple them with a spray-gun handle and you have a great way to practice spraying without having to worry about gun setup, fluid thickness, or air pressure. The handle makes the can easier to control, less tiring, and closer to the feeling of a spray gun. These inexpensive plastic trigger handles are generally sold in the same section as the spray cans and cost about $3.

A trigger handle for a spray can creates a close approximation of what spraying with a gun is like. Buying premixed colored lacquers solves the problems of mixing colors, fluid viscosity, and air pressure.

Where to Spray

When you spray, a lot of finish and solvent misses the wood or bounces back off. It ends up as airborne mist called "overspray." To prevent the overspray from settling on everything in your shop, including you and your lungs, you must spray where there is excellent ventilation. The two options are outdoors and in a spray booth. Outdoors is pretty self-explanatory; it is a wide open area with plenty of air movement and the added disadvantage of lots of dust, spores, and leaves. A spray booth is an air funnel with

Is it possible to spray oil-based varnish?

Although varnish is formulated for brushing, you can spray it. Choose a thick varnish and reduce it 50/50 with acetone. The acetone will allow it to spray easily and will flash off very quickly. Spray a very light mist on the entire piece, wait about 5 minutes for the solvents to flash off, then spray a thin wet coat. The mist coat will help the wet coat hang without running. One more thing: Except for the top, which will be horizontal, spray the rest of the piece upside down. That way, if you do get some sags or runs, they will be far less obvious after you turn the piece right side up again.

a fan at the small end and the sprayer (you) at the large end.

In order to spray flammable materials, like solvent-borne finishes, you must have an explosion-proof booth that meets the fire codes for your locality. See your local fire marshall and insurance company about what you need for spraying these coatings. However, if you are only going to spray nonflammable materials, like water-borne coatings, you can set up a simple spray booth with a box fan, a bit of cardboard, and some creativity.

A simple window booth For spraying small pieces that will fit on top of my workbench, I've devised an inexpensive spray booth that fits in my shop window. I started with a 20-in. box fan in the window, turned on its side so that I can reach the speed controls after the cardboard is in place. I made a three-sided shroud out of stiff cardboard that essentially turns the fan into an air-moving funnel (see the drawing below).

For a 20-in. fan, start with a strip of cardboard about 18 in. wide. Cut three

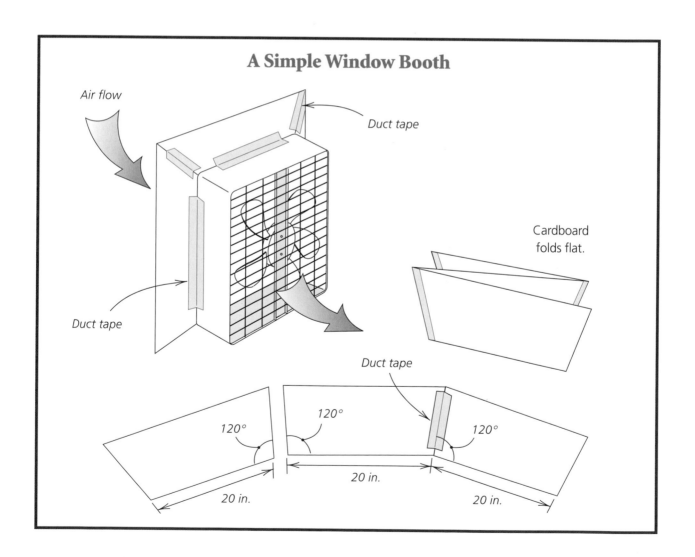

A Simple Window Booth

Air flow

Duct tape

Duct tape

Cardboard folds flat.

Duct tape

120°

120°

120°

20 in.

20 in.

20 in.

trapezoids with the short side 20 in. long and each end angled away from one another at 120°. Tape them together along the angled edges with duct tape. Fold them at the taped edges so that the small sides create a 20-in. by 20-in. opening, which you then tape onto the frame of the fan toward the front edge. You should now have a three-sided cardboard funnel with a fan at the small end blowing out of the window. Tape a 20-in. by 20-in. furnace filter onto the front grill to keep the fan clean of overspray (see the photo at left below).

Since my window is just above my workbench, I use the bench as a surface to hold the piece I will spray. To protect the bench, I cover it with cardboard, brown paper, or plastic. I place the piece to be sprayed on a small turntable so that I can turn the piece around without having to touch it (see the photo at right below). It is important that you always spray toward the fan so that the overspray goes outside.

Fold the panels at the duct-tape hinges to make a shroud and tape it onto the top and two sides of the fan. Tape a filter in front of the fan and place the unit in an open window in the shop.

Use your benchtop or a table under the window to support the piece you are spraying. This homemade turntable sits atop protective cardboard and lets the author turn this wet bowl without touching it.

A collapsible garage booth For spraying larger pieces, I have a larger booth. Like the window booth, it is inexpensive, made primarily of cardboard and duct tape, and it folds flat to store in my plywood rack (see the photo at right below). I set it up in front of an open garage door with a ½-hp fan blowing out.

This booth is a five-sided funnel with a lid. The lid is 30 in. wide and 8 ft. long with a 1-in. by 1-in. beam along the front edge. It hooks onto the walls of the booth with hook-and-loop fastener tabs. By changing where the side walls hook onto the lid I can change the size and taper of the funnel. The back wall and two of the four side walls are panels of 4-ft. by 6-ft. cardboard taped at the edges with duct tape. Two smaller 2-ft.-wide walls act as wings to add extra versatility and extend the depth of the booth. The back wall has a cutout to accept a ½-hp fan, which is covered with filter cloth to keep overspray off its blades.

Set up the booth in front of an open garage door. You can change the size and taper of the booth by moving the side walls in or out. The lid, stiffened with an 8-ft.-long beam, holds the walls in position with hook-and-loop fasteners. This booth is powered by a ½-hp exhaust fan. The blue filter cloth also attaches with hook-and-loop fasteners so that it completely covers the grill.

When the spraying is done, the booth folds flat and stores in the plywood rack alongside the dismantled turntable. The booth goes up or down in under 5 minutes.

A Collapsible Garage Booth

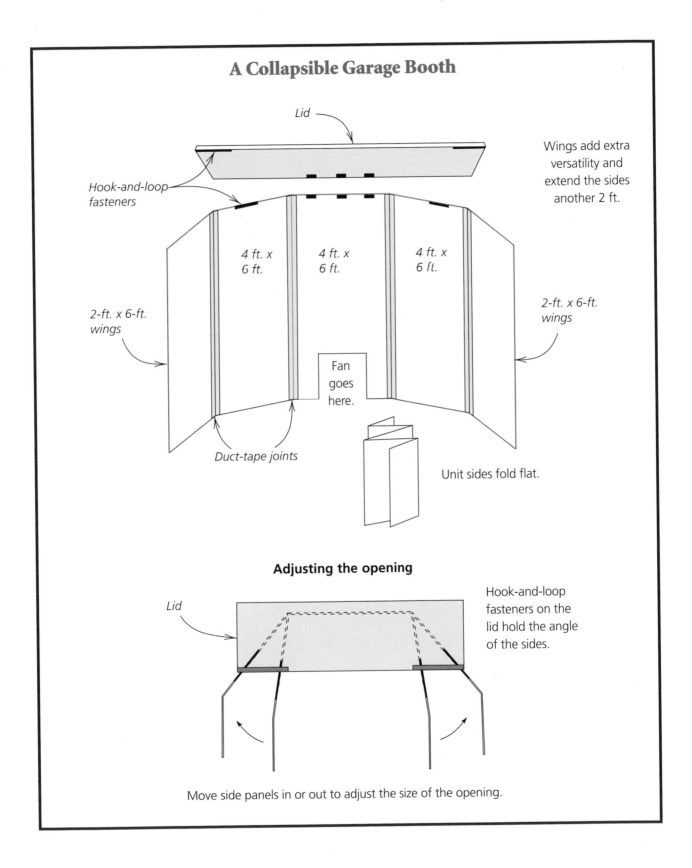

Lid

Hook-and-loop
fasteners

Wings add extra
versatility and
extend the sides
another 2 ft.

4 ft. x
6 ft.

4 ft. x
6 ft.

4 ft. x
6 ft.

2-ft. x 6-ft.
wings

2-ft. x 6-ft.
wings

Fan
goes
here.

Duct-tape joints

Unit sides fold flat.

Adjusting the opening

Lid

Hook-and-loop
fasteners on the
lid hold the angle
of the sides.

Move side panels in or out to adjust the size of the opening.

Spray in the direction of the airflow (toward the fan, covered in blue filter material) so that you are in clean air and the mist-laden air goes away from you. To spray the other side of a piece, you'll need to turn it. That is where a spray booth turntable comes in handy. Here the author sprays a chair on his homemade turntable.

To set up the turntable, screw the pipes into their flanges, slip the 1-in. pipe inside the 1¼-in. pipe until the upper flange rests on the edge of the larger pipe. Give the top disk a spin, and you have a heavy-duty turntable, just over 2 ft. high, that is stable, inexpensive, and stores away in just a few minutes.

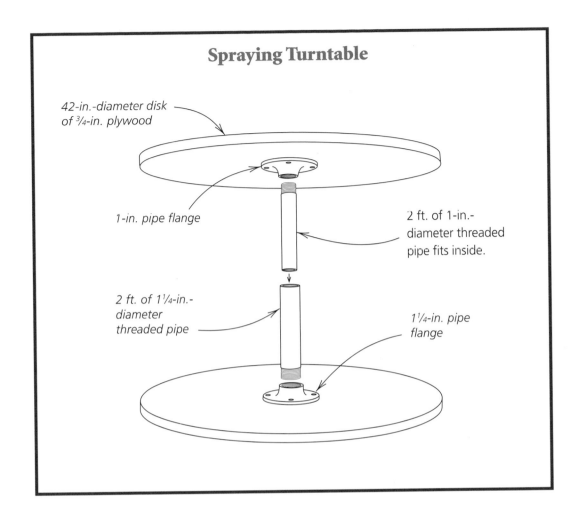

Spraying Turntable

42-in.-diameter disk of ¾-in. plywood

1-in. pipe flange

2 ft. of 1-in.-diameter threaded pipe fits inside.

2 ft. of 1¼-in.-diameter threaded pipe

1¼-in. pipe flange

A spraying turntable If you are going to spray, you need a turntable. The reason is simple. For the booth to work, you have to spray into it and toward the fan, not away from it. If you can spray in only one direction, you must turn the piece you are spraying around in order to hit the other side. It is pretty difficult to do that once the piece is mostly wet with finish. A turntable is just the ticket.

The one I use is made from a sheet of ¾-in. plywood and two pieces of 2-ft. threaded pipe, two flanges, and some screws. Cut two 42-in. disks from the plywood sheet. Buy a 2-ft. section of threaded 1-in.-diameter pipe, and another of 1¼-in.-diameter pipe. Attach a 1-in. pipe flange to the center of one disk and a 1¼-in. flange to the center of the other. Screw the pipes into the flange, add a bit of grease on the open edge of the larger pipe, and slide the smaller pipe inside the large one (see the photo at right on the facing page). It should fit with very little play, and the top disk should spin easily while the bottom one acts as a base to the

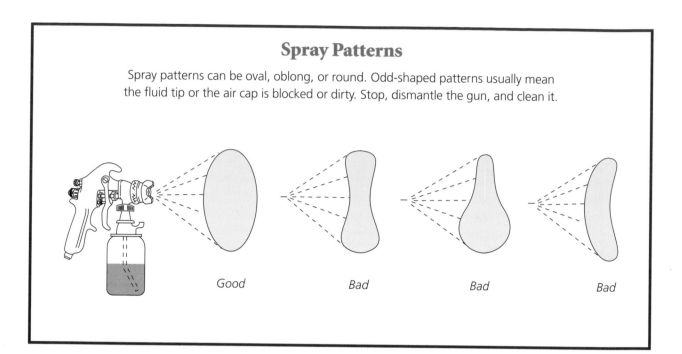

Spray Patterns

Spray patterns can be oval, oblong, or round. Odd-shaped patterns usually mean the fluid tip or the air cap is blocked or dirty. Stop, dismantle the gun, and clean it.

Good

Bad

Bad

Bad

Currently I'm building two plywood bookcases. The only place I have to spray them is in the basement of a church. The room is large (50 ft. wide by 80 ft. long by 16 ft. high) and is heated to about 65°F. The closest point of a pilot light is 80 ft. from the area I would use. There would be no ventilation other than what occurs normally. In this large room can I use lacquer without fear of an explosion (I can spread the work over several days if required)?

Nope. And "ventilation that occurs normally" is inadequate unless "normally" means that the doors and windows are open and a stiff breeze is going through. OSHA mandates air movement of 100 fpm (feet per minute) across the square footage of the face of a booth. A booth large enough to do this unit would therefore draw about 3600 cfm (cubic feet per minute) of air. Does the natural ventilation in the room do this? If not, you are heading toward both an explosion and a breathing hazard.

turntable. When it is time to put the turntable away, simply unscrew the pipes from their flanges and pack the unit away flat.

Solvent-Borne Finishes

Solvent-borne finishes, like lacquer, shellac, conversion varnish, and catalyzed lacquer, are flammable and explosive and require an explosion-proof spray booth. But once you get beyond the equipment problems, these are some of the easiest finishes to spray.

Before you pull the trigger, picture a spray pattern that will enable you to cover all parts of the piece evenly and uniformly. Check the gun's setup by spraying first on a piece of scrap wood or cardboard. The spray pattern should be uniform and correctly shaped (oval, oblong, or round).

FINISHING TALES

Old Paint

The reason Gary and I became such fast friends is that one day he found me singing in the spray booth.

A spray booth is a noisy place. With the compressor running, the exhaust fan on, and the air whooshing through the gun, you can't hear anything but yourself. There is a delightful sense of seclusion. So even though I'm a lousy singer, I could warble at the top of my lungs with relative impunity, knowing that the din of the booth would protect others from my awful singing.

Of course, I had a reason for singing. Spraying is a very rhythmic activity. A good sprayer has to keep constantly in motion to apply a consistently smooth, even coating. A slight pause will usually translate into a run or sag, and a change in gun speed will mean a variance in film thickness. To maintain a constant fluid motion, I'd pace myself by singing as I sprayed.

Apparently, I wasn't the only one, for when Gary wandered in and discovered my secret, he ad-mitted that he did the same thing. I knew then and there that he must be a good finisher, and I was right—he was. That's why it was so surprising when our job went haywire.

We had contracted to refinish six guitar bodies, matching the color to the original specs. To guard against contamination, we decided to seal them first with two coats of shellac. As shellac ages, it turns rubbery, so we always mixed our own fresh. I found a full jug of shellac in the spray room, but I couldn't re-member how old it was, so I mixed another and left it on a small table near the booth. Since we always used the same 1-qt. juice bottles to mix the shellac flakes with alcohol, we never bothered to label them.

By Friday, Gary had the gui-tars sealed, sanded, and ready for the color coat. It was one of those rare days when everything goes right, and I had hit the color quickly without having to tweak the mixture until I had 2 gal. too many. In fact, when the spraying was done, we had less than 6 oz. of extra color left. We left for the weekend with light hearts.

As usual, Gary was in first Monday morning. "Better go look in the booth," he grunted. The guitars looked like mud flats with big plate-like cracks where the shrinking lacquer had split over the shellac. As I stood in shock wondering what could have gone wrong, my eye fell on the still full jar of shellac I had mixed the week before. Not far away was the jug of old material—empty.

Our momentum on that job never recovered. It took far longer to refinish those guitars the second time, and we ended up with about a gallon of extra topcoat as we kept adding more in an attempt to get the color right. Gary stored the extra col-ored lacquer on a shelf with one of his hand-drawn labels on the can. The drawing on the label was an American Indian astride a pony, with the label "Old Paint."

Spraying Technique

For even coverage, spray with the gun held at a constant distance
from the wood (top); do not move it in and out in an arc pattern (bottom).

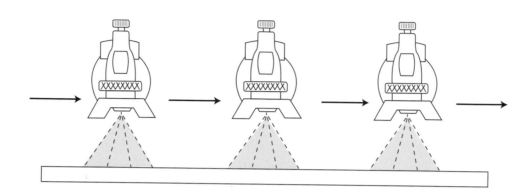

Even application

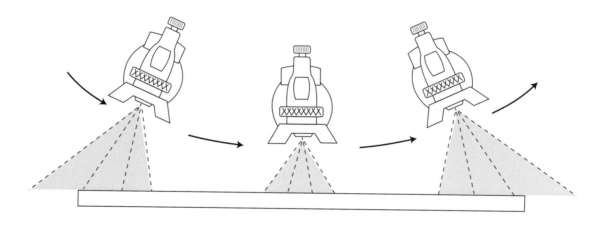

Light application   *Heavy application*   *Light application*

You might want to take a few practice passes with the finish on scrap so that you know how much finish is coming out and how fast you will have to move the gun.

Try to keep the gun about 8 in. from the wood and move parallel to the wood's surface. Don't swing back and forth in arcs, or you will end up with centers that are too wet and ends that are too dry (see the drawing on the facing page). Admittedly, that is easier to describe than to do, but with a bit of practice it will come naturally. Pull the trigger just before the gun arrives at the wood's edge and hold it until just after you pass the far edge. Keep the gun moving, or you will end up with a run or a puddle.

On each pass of the gun, make the spray pattern overlap one-half to two-thirds of the last pass (see the drawing on p. 145). If you don't overlap enough, you can end up with wide bands of wetter and drier finish on the surface.

If the finish goes on too thick, leaving an orange-peel pattern or overspray, you may need to thin the material with extra solvent. For the best results, don't spray on too much. It is better to spray several light, thin coats than one heavy coat. Each thin coat of material will dry quickly, usually within 10 minutes. Unless the material is very thin, stick to a maximum of two or three coats per day. Shellac and lacquer do not have to be sanded between coats, no matter how long they have had

I sprayed catalyzed lacquer on an entertainment center, and as the finish cured it developed cracks. What caused this and how can I fix it?

Assuming that you built up the finish from the raw wood using only catalyzed lacquers and sealers, the cracking may be due to one of three factors. The first is "violating the window." These coatings generally have a "recoat window"—a period of time during which it is safe to recoat. This should be clearly spelled out on the technical data sheet that most companies make available with their coatings. If you recoat too soon, or in some cases too late, you can create these problems.

The second possibility is a faulty mixture. The lacquer "cross-links" (or catalyzes) due to the action of an acid that you must add to the lacquer prior to spraying. The acid must be measured out exactly and not estimated—putting in the wrong amount can cause anything from a minor change in sheen or "gloss" to the cracking you describe.

The third possibility is a coating that is too thick. Catalyzed lacquers and sealers are designed for two or three coats at most, and building up many coats can also cause cracking.

Now for the bad news. There is only one way to repair it: Strip off the coating and refinish the piece. You cannot chemically "re-knit" catalyzed lacquer.

Spray Troubleshooting

Problem	Cause	Solution
Blush	Humidity is too high.	Respray with retarder or slow solvent added.
Overspray	1. Spray is too dry. 2. Incoming air pressure is too low. 3. Not enough coating exits gun.	1. Thin material or spray wetter coat. 2. Increase or decrease air pressure. 3. Increase fluid flow by turning fluid regulator knob counter-clockwise.
Orange peel	Material is too thick.	Thin coating.
Bands	Not enough overlap in spray pattern.	Overlap each pass by two-thirds.

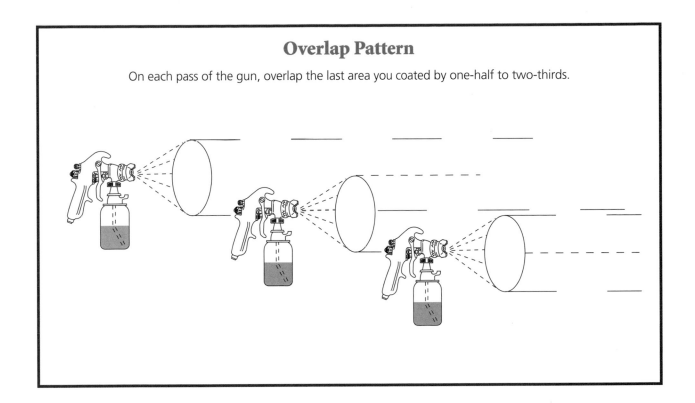

Overlap Pattern

On each pass of the gun, overlap the last area you coated by one-half to two-thirds.

to dry. Catalyzed lacquer and conversion varnish must be sanded (with 320-grit self-lubricating paper) if it has been more than six hours since the previous coat was applied.

Waterborne Coatings

Spray guns must have stainless-steel fluid passageways to spray waterbornes because steel ones rust. I have found that waterbornes atomize best when the gun is fitted with a smaller fluid aperture. The standard aperture for solvent-borne coatings is 0.070 in. (1.75mm), but waterbornes do better with a 0.040-in. (1mm)

opening. Fluid tips are usually sold as a package, which may include the tip, needle, and air cap as a set. Your gun manufacturer can steer you to the right setup.

The homemade booths described on pp. 134-140 work for spraying nonflammable waterborne coatings. The coatings are generally ready to spray and need no thinning. As a rule, spray lighter and thinner than you think you should. Waterbornes should be sprayed so that the surface is barely wet. More than that and they are likely to run and sag. Practice first on scrap and spray no more than two coats per day.

Repairing
Damage

Finish repair really consists of only three things: removing excess materials, like debris, drips, and runs; filling voids, like chips, dents, and pinholes; and changing colors that don't match, which is called touchup. Drips, runs, and debris are a function of finishing. They are hard to avoid, but occur only while you are applying a finish and not afterward. Chips, dents, rubs, and pinholes, on the other hand, may occur during handling but are also a lifelong bane of finished pieces. Doping in, burn in, and touchup are used to address chips, dents, and rubs.

Removing Excess Materials

It would certainly be nice if all our finishing efforts resulted in smooth, defect-free surfaces, but it doesn't usually happen that way. More often than not the surface sports a variety of protrusions that stick out above the nice, level plane we were seeking. Sometimes they are beyond our control. Nature provides lots of airborne debris ready to land in our wet finishes. At other times, we are responsible for our own problems by accidentally creating drips, runs, and sags. Either way, if it sticks out above the surface, we need to remove it.

Debris
Wet finishes have the unfortunate knack of collecting all sorts of airborne debris. If something big, like an errant bug, gets into the finish, it is best to pluck it out while the coating is still wet and hope the finish flows into the void. If not, or if you don't catch it in time, you will have to dig it out after the finish is dry and deal

with the resulting hole as a void to be filled. Small dust and dirt particles that settle into the drying film, on the other hand, will usually only result in small pimples in the dried finish. These will almost always flatten and disappear during the light sanding stage of the rubbing process described in Chapter 9. If you are planning to rub out the finish, and you should, don't worry about these small nibs.

Drips and Runs

Drips and runs—and a version of runs known as "curtains," the wide sags that form on vertical surfaces—take more work than debris. If the drips, runs, or curtains are the result of spraying, or if you don't catch them immediately while brushing, you must wait until they dry completely to fix them. Because they are thicker than the rest of the finish, they will take longer to dry. If you try to cut or sand them too soon, they are likely to peel right down to the raw wood. It will usually take several days—and possibly more—for runs to dry sufficiently. Test the run by pressing your nail into the thickest part (see the top photo at right). If it gives easily, let it dry some more. Even after the runs dry, you'll find that the repair methods that work best on brittle finishes are different from those that work best for flexible ones.

Brittle finishes Drips, runs, and curtains on brittle finishes, like shellac, lacquer, and most waterbornes, dry hard in just a few days. They usually shrink substantially during that time and won't look as bad

Press your thumbnail into the bulb of a drip to see if it is dry enough to repair. If it takes an impression, give it more time to dry.

On brittle finishes like shellac, lacquer, and most waterbornes, use a razor blade like a tiny scraper to remove the excess material.

as when they were new. Level them with a single-edge razor blade used like a tiny scraper held at 90° to the surface (see the bottom photo above). Scrape off the bulk of the drip or run so that the surface is level. You can do the last bit of leveling

Witness Lines

On occasion you will sand through the last coat of finish into the one below. This is not a problem with the brittle evaporative finishes, which redissolve themselves and form one thick coating. But with waterborne coatings and reactive finishes, like varnish and polyurethane, it is common for a faint outline to show where one coat has been sanded through to a previous coat. These outlines are called "halos" or "witness lines."

These faint outlines where a coat of finish is sanded through to a previous coat cannot be blended with sanding or rubbing. More sanding or rubbing with abrasive compounds only makes them larger. If you get a witness line while sanding out a defect or while sanding prior to rubbing to satin or gloss, stop as soon as you see it forming. Clean off any soap, rubbing compound, or wax you are using as a rubbing lubricant, and resand the entire piece lightly with 320-grit self-lubricating paper. Once you have sanded, apply another thin coat of finish.

Witness Lines

Sanding through one coat of a reactive finish to the previous coat may result in a faint, but visible outline, called a "witness line."

Side view

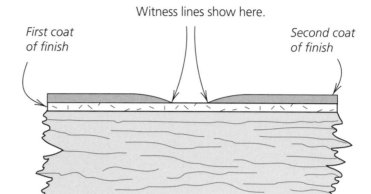

Witness lines show here.

First coat of finish

Second coat of finish

Top view

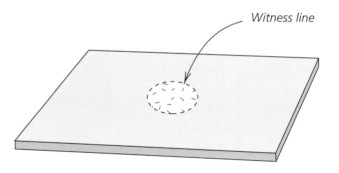

Witness line

with 600-grit sandpaper wrapped around a small sanding block and lubricated with some soapy water. Don't try to sand out the whole run, though, or you will probably cut through the surrounding area down to the wood.

If the drip or run is in the final coat and you remove it without cutting through to the wood, you can go directly to rubbing or polishing after you have leveled it. Otherwise, remove any soap residue with a clean damp cloth, and when the surface is dry, move on to your next coat.

Flexible finishes Oil-based coatings, like varnish and polyurethane, along with many waterborne polyurethanes, are more flexible. Runs don't shrink as much and they dry far slower. You may have to wait a week or more to repair them. They won't get brittle, but the runs will get very hard and rubbery. At that point, cut off the run with a new single-edge razor blade held at a very low angle—almost flat against the surface, as shown in the photo at right.

Once the bulk of the run is off, wet-sand the area with 600-grit wet/dry paper, a small sanding block, and some soapy water as a lubricant. If the run is in the final coat, go ahead and rub it out. If it's not, clean off the soap, scuff the area with 320-grit paper, and recoat.

I spilled some perfume on my lacquered vanity. It was wiped up quickly, but it etched the surface, and the lacquer is no longer shiny where the perfume was. How can I repair this?

Since the finish is more or less intact, you can simply repolish the surface to make it shiny again. Go to an auto parts store and buy some automotive polishing compound. It is available in a gel packaged in a flat round tin or in liquid form in a squeeze bottle. Put a bit of compound on a damp cotton cloth and rub vigorously. In a few minutes the surface of the cloth will be dry and the finish will have a cloudy haze where the compound has dried. Buff it off and you should have your gloss lacquer back again.

On a flexible finish, such as oil-based varnish or polyurethane, slice off the run with a razor blade held at a very low angle.

or a very fine brush, place a drop or two of finish into the void (see the drawing on the facing page). At first it will be higher than the surrounding surface, but as it dries it will shrink below the surface. Once it is dry, go back and add another drop, and continue until the dried surface is slightly above the surrounding area.

Once the area has been filled, sand it perfectly smooth with 600-grit wet/dry paper wrapped around a small sanding block. Use some soapy water as a lubricant. If you feel there is enough finish to rub, you can usually rub out the surface to satin or gloss so that the spot disappears. On the other hand, if the finish is too thin, clean off any soap residue, scuff-sand lightly with 320-grit self-lubricating paper, and add another coat of finish.

Filling Voids

Chips and dents are usually the result of accidental dings when handling finished pieces. These often occur when we are assembling or moving pieces we've just made, but they also show up after the furniture starts getting use. Pinholes are areas where finish is missing due to a rising air bubble or a small void in the wood. Whether the problem is in a newly applied finish or one that has been in service for a while, the repair is the same. If there is finish missing, we have to replace it, and the best thing to replace it with is more finish. The two ways to do that are by doping in and by burning in.

Doping In

The process of gradually filling in a void with drops of the same finish is called doping in or kootching. With a toothpick

Burning In

Burning in is the process of filling finish defects with hot-melt resins that look and act like clear, colored, or tinted finish. Unlike doping in, which requires several applications of replacement finish and lots of drying time, burning in takes only minutes and the surface is ready to work almost immediately. It also works on almost any finish, so you can burn in on an older piece if you don't have that finish on hand. But there is a trade-off. The technique requires some skill and practice along with specialized equipment and materials (see the photo on p. 152).

Burn-in sticks are bars of solid lacquer made to melt at a fairly low temperature,

Doping In

1 Place a drop of finish into the void.

2 At first, the finish will sit above the surrounding surface.

3 As the finish dries, it will shrink below the surface. Continue to add drops, letting each one dry completely, until the void is filled when dry.

4 Once it is sanded, the spot should be completely flush with the surrounding surface.

flow into a defect, and reharden as they cool. The sticks come in a variety of solid and transparent colors as well as clear. Because they are heat sensitive, it is best to store them in a cool place, such as the refrigerator. When the sticks get too hot or too old, they develop a fine crack pattern on the surface, and instead of flowing when you melt them, they get gummy. When that happens, toss them and buy new ones.

You can melt the sticks with anything that gets hot enough to make them flow, such as a soldering iron or woodburning tool. However, there are commercial knives that give you more control over both the amount of heat you generate and the shape and size of the knife. I like to work with a small electric oven that heats the knives, and with two different blades: one shaped like a grapefruit knife and the other—called a dragaway knife—with a flat surface for scraping repairs level. The right temperature is important for burning in. If the knife is too hot, the stick will bubble and may leave pinholes in the

A variety of burn-in knives are heated in an oven until they are hot enough to melt the lacquer sticks (right). Different-shape knives excel at filling small voids or scraping surfaces flat.

repair (see the photo at left below). It can also burn the surrounding finish. If it is too cold, it simply won't melt the stick.

Here's how I do it. First, I choose a stick that is the color of the lightest background color in the wood. If I don't have the right color, I go lighter, never darker. I melt a small amount of stick, no bigger than a BB, on the end of the hot knife and press it into the void quickly. If I need more, I repeat the process. I fill the same way I would dope in; just enough to fill slightly above level. With the flat of the heated dragaway knife, I lightly scrape any excess to make the burn-in flush with the finish. Be careful, since a hot knife can easily burn or move finish. At first, you might want to border the repair with tape to protect the surrounding surface (see the photo on p. 154). When it is done right, the repair should feel flush. In just seconds it will be cool and hard.

Once the repair is dry, sand it very lightly with 600-grit wet/dry paper and a bit of mineral spirits as a lubricant. It should take very little sanding, and when

If the knife is too hot, like the one in this photo, the burn-in stick will bubble, leaving air bubbles in the repair.

In this photo the knife is the right temperature to melt the burn-in stick without bubbling it. By melting only a small amount of stick at a time, you can fill a void without destroying the surrounding finish.

To protect the surrounding finish when burning in, you can mask off the area with tape.

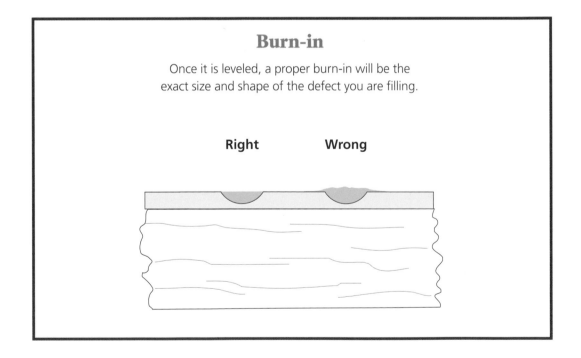

Burn-in

Once it is leveled, a proper burn-in will be the
exact size and shape of the defect you are filling.

Right   **Wrong**

If the color is rubbed off but the grain is still intact, "stain" the area with a wash of pigment or dye mixed into the touchup shellac.

it is leveled, the fill should be the original shape of the defect.

Burning in is one of the more skilled tasks in finishing. Make sure you practice on finished scrap wood before you attempt it on that heirloom breakfront.

Touchup

Whether it is on a patch filled with putty, a burn-in, or an area where color was rubbed off, touchup consists of painting a convincing picture of wood on a repaired or worn area. It can be as simple as restaining an area where the wood pattern shows but the stain color has worn off (see the photo above), or it can be as complicated as re-creating all the subtle grain, color, and figure that wood sports.

Wood is not one color, but rather a mixture of hues that our eye averages into

Can I use conventional lacquer burn-in sticks and methods to repair a polyurethane finish?

Yes. You can even French polish over polyurethane to build up worn areas and restore sheen.

How do I remove ink stains from a finish?

You don't. They almost never come out. Many inks have the same solvent as many finishes, and if the ink is in the finish, expect it to stay there until you refinish.

one general tone. If you look closely at wood, you will see that even a small spot contains a wide range of colors, pores, and patterns. Wood is also semi-translucent and gives the effect of depth as you view its patterns. Putty or burn-in spots are one solid color, and they are largely

A squeeze bottle of thin shellac, some fine sable brushes, a glass mixing palette, and a box of finely ground pigment powders make a complete touchup kit.

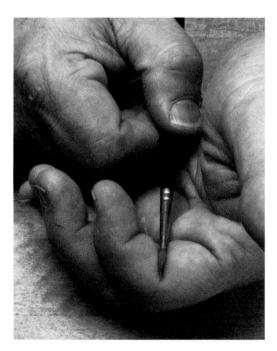

Dip the brush in shellac and reshape it in the crook of your finger.

opaque. To make them look like the surrounding wood you must paint on a convincing pattern of wood grain and layers of translucent colors. That is why I said always to burn in with a color as light as or lighter than the lightest background color in the wood. It is easy to make a spot darker, but virtually impossible to make it lighter.

Like burning in, touchup calls for a specialized set of materials. I mix my "paints" by adding powdered pigments or dyes to thin shellac. A piece of glass or mirror is the perfect mixing palette, since it is colorless and easy to clean. Good brushes allow me full control over my work, and my "color box" keeps the pigments organized. You can choose your own work tools, but to start you off, here are my recommendations.

My favorite touchup brushes are fine Kolinsky sable in small sizes, from 00 up to 4. These brushes consistently shape to a very fine point that allows you to paint in even the most subtle grain lines. The bristles should shape naturally to a sharp point and be flexible and springy. Expect to spend $10 to $20 or more per brush for good-quality sables.

To keep the brushes in good shape indefinitely, I follow a strict cleaning and storage ritual. I clean them in alcohol (the solvent for shellac), then dip them into clean shellac. I reshape the tip in the crook of my finger (see the bottom photo on the facing page) and store them bristles up in a cup so that nothing but air touches the tip. The shellac dries to form a shell that protects the bristles and keeps them shaped until I am ready to use them again. I then dip them in alcohol, which dissolves the shellac, and I am ready to work.

My color box is a slab of wood with a series of stop-holes drilled into it and a hinged lid (see the top photo on the facing page). I've filled the holes with a range of finely ground dry pigment powders sold especially for touchup work. The colors are arranged in logical order from light to dark. A few extra holes on the right contain alcohol-soluble dyes, for when I need transparent colors. Avoid using dyes if you will be recoating the touchup with another coat of finish. The

First paint in the fine grain and ray lines with pigment, shellac, and a small, pointed touchup brush. (If you do the background color first you are likely to end up too dark.)

Then fill in the background colors with short strokes of different hues or a semi-transparent wash of color. Make a wash by mixing only a little bit of pigment or dye into the shellac.

dyes sometimes bleed up into the finish, changing the color in the process.

You can buy brushes at any good art supply store. For other touchup materials, see Resources on p. 175.

When you have all your materials lined up, you're ready to start the touchup process. Begin with the grain lines, then add the background colors (see the photos above). By breaking up the patch with

FINISHING TALES

The Old Shell Game

"In-house" repair work is about as far from glamorous as you can get, but it pays well, and the locale changes every day. This home, however, was one that spelled trouble the minute we walked in. Mrs. Needleman had already convinced herself that the water damage on her table was not repairable, in spite of anything we could say or do.

The water mark was caused by a plant that had been sitting on one of two identical end tables that bracketed the living-room couch. Because the tables were a matched set, the owner did not want to refinish one for fear that the set would no longer match. We assured her that we could get the white ring out completely, but her skepticism outranked our powers of persuasion.

My boss Nat convinced Mrs. Needleman to leave the house for two hours because the materials we would be using were quite offensive. There are few things more annoying than having someone watch over your shoulder while you are working on their precious furniture. And in this case, the actual repair would take only a few minutes,

and he was sure she would object to the fee charged if she found out how easy the job was.

Once the owner left, we moved the lamp off the table and set to work. It took only a few quick swipes with alcohol to get the water mark completely out, and a light polish with paste wax restored the sheen to the top. Within 15 minutes, the top was perfect, and no sign remained of its water mark. To make sure that the sheen on the two tables matched, we decided to wax the other one as well. That's when Nat hatched his fiendishly simple plot.

We switched the tables.

The table that had recently been cured of its water mark went into the far corner, and the undamaged one took its place. That way, when Mrs. Needleman scrutinized our "repair," she was sure to be satisfied. After carefully replacing the lamps, we sat down on the couch and Nat regaled me with stories of previous jobs.

When we heard the door open, we both jumped up from the couch and assumed our work positions. When Mrs. Needleman walked in, she saw me assiduous-

ly polishing what she assumed was the repaired table while Nat packed our tools. In reality, the polishing rag was dry and the table was an impostor.

"Well, what do you think?" asked Nat as he pointed to the phony "repaired" table. Mrs. Needleman turned on the lamp and started studying the top. She crouched, turned, and looked at it from every angle as we watched in silence. Finally, she gave her verdict. "Hmm..., It's a very good job, boys. Of course, I can still see a faint ring where the water mark was, but really, it's just fine. After all, one can't expect perfection, right?"

"Right," replied Nat as he handed her the bill, grinning smugly. Just as we had planned, none of us even looked at the real repair job.

We never heard from Mrs. Needleman, even though I am certain that she discovered our ploy. How do I know we were found out? The tables were the square, boxy type with a drawer for storage. And we hadn't bothered to switch the contents of the drawers.

lines of color, you can easily fool the eye. Not yours, of course. You will always be able to spot your own touchup, but you will be surprised how easy it is to fool others. Don't be afraid to be creative with your repairs. I'll sometimes add grain lines on oak or pitch pockets on cherry to hide defects. I've even been known to add an extra fake knot on knotty pine, as shown in the photos below.

I have an old family heirloom table that has water rings on the surface. How do I go about repairing this without messing up the finish? Do I need to completely refinish the whole top?

You can almost always remove water rings with a quick wipe of alcohol. Put denatured alcohol on a soft rag and wring it out. You want the rag damp with alcohol, but not wet—about as damp as a healthy dog's nose. Swipe the damp rag over the area quickly once or twice. The water rings should come out immediately.

On knotty wood, you can hide a repair by painting in a fake knot over it.

The added knot (left) looks similar enough to the real one (right) to fool the casual observer.

Rubbing Out the Finish

It is almost impossible to apply a finish and have it end up completely smooth. Odds are, you will have some orange peel, brush marks, marks from shrinkage, or dust and dirt nibs, all of which can be seen and felt. Simply by rubbing the finish, you can convert it to one that is completely level and feels smooth and silky.

Virtually any finish can be rubbed provided it is adequately cured and is thick enough so that it doesn't come off completely during the rubbing process. The rubbing process is essentially the same no matter what the finish is. Of course, some materials rub easier, faster, or glossier than others. Generally speaking, brittle finishes will rub to a higher gloss more easily than more flexible finishes.

Very thin wipe-on finishes, like oil, Danish oil, wipe-on gel, and even French polish, won't need to be rubbed. Those finishes don't gather dust, are not prone to brush marks or orange peel, and frankly, are too thin to be rubbed anyway. But most other finishes can be either rubbed to satin or polished to gloss. I have often heard people describe satin finishes as "softer" and "more natural looking" and gloss finishes as "brighter, shinier, and more glasslike." Technically, the only difference is that gloss finishes reflect more light than satin finishes.

As a general rule, it is only necessary to rub easily seen flat surfaces, particularly horizontal ones, like tabletops or shelves. However, door fronts are also candidates. I also rub chairs or any item that will be

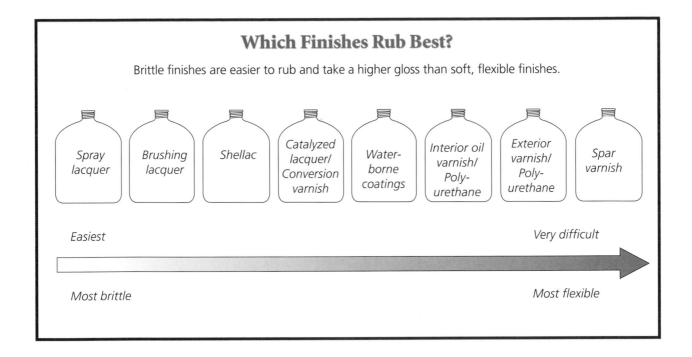

Which Finishes Rub Best?

Brittle finishes are easier to rub and take a higher gloss than soft, flexible finishes.

Spray lacquer | Brushing lacquer | Shellac | Catalyzed lacquer/Conversion varnish | Water-borne coatings | Interior oil varnish/Poly-urethane | Exterior varnish/Poly-urethane | Spar varnish

Easiest → Very difficult

Most brittle → Most flexible

handled, but not the underside of tables or hidden areas on cabinets. If you are prefinishing, you can rub all the inside areas of a cabinet or shelves. Some may call it overkill, but it is an easy way to add an impressive level of craftsmanship.

What Is Rubbing?

The object of rubbing a finish is to flatten the surface and remove small dust particles, brush marks, shrink marks, and orange peel. Therefore, the rubbing process is an abrasive one—it removes finish (see the drawing on p. 162). When you get done, you will end up with a thinner finish than when you started, so it is important to make sure the finish is thick enough before you rub. A good starting point is at least 6 mils thick before rub-

bing. (A mil is 0.001 in.—one thousandth of an inch. For purposes of comparison, this page is about 4 mils thick.) A satin rub will usually remove about 1 mil, more or less, and a gloss rub as much as 2 to 3 mils.

Cutting through to a previous coat is not usually a problem with lacquer or shellac, because each coat remelts the ones before it. But with varnish, poly-urethane, and waterborne coatings, which do not melt in, cutting through to a previous layer can leave a witness line, an outline showing the interface of the two layers (see p. 148). If you are working on a glazed finish, where some of the color is "floated" between layers instead of stained into the wood, be careful not to cut through a layer of color, because it will leave a light-colored patch.

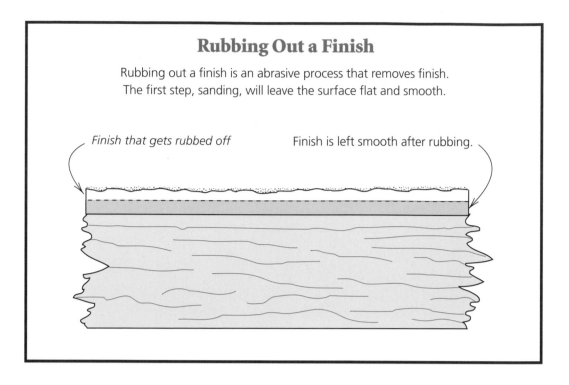

Rubbing Out a Finish

Rubbing out a finish is an abrasive process that removes finish.
The first step, sanding, will leave the surface flat and smooth.

Finish that gets rubbed off

Finish is left smooth after rubbing.

Now that I know what witness lines are, I also know I have them. I rubbed some waterborne polyurethane, and now I have a line where I cut through the top layer into the second. It's quite visible. Is there any way to hide it, or do I need to refinish?

You do NOT need to refinish. You may be able to hide the lines, but if not, the worst-case scenario is that you may have to apply one more coat of finish.

You can sometimes hide witness lines by carefully rubbing to satin finish. Lightly sand the area with 1000-grit paper, then rub the area around the witness lines with 0000 steel wool. Now, go back and rub the entire surface. At times, this will make the witness lines almost invisible.

If not, clean off any wax from the rubbing process with naphtha, wipe it clean, scuff the surface with 320-grit paper, and apply at least one more coat of the waterborne polyurethane. Leave plenty of dry time, and this time when you sand or rub it, be more gentle. Often the difference between cutting through and not cutting through has to do with how well the last coat lays out. If you apply a good, smooth final coat, you won't have to sand as much.

In addition to flattening and removing debris, rubbing leaves a scratch pattern on the now-level surface. The difference between a finish rubbed to satin and one taken to gloss is merely the size and depth of the scratches. You can continue rubbing a finish from satin to gloss simply by graduating to finer and finer polishing compounds in the same way you go from coarser- to finer-grit sandpaper.

The small scratches control how much light is reflected off the viewed surface of the wood and how much is deflected. Reflected light bounces off a surface at the same angle but opposite direction from where it enters. Deflected light bounces off the surface in any angle or direction (see the drawing on p. 164). A glossier surface reflects more; a flatter satin surface

How to Tell How Thick the Finish Is

It is all well and good to say that the finish needs to be 6 mils thick (0.006 in.) in order to rub it. But how do you know how much finish is on the wood?

Devices that measure dry mil thickness without destroying the finish do exist, but they are quite expensive (upward of $3,000). To measure wet finish, a cheaper ($2) gizmo called a wet film thickness gauge works (see the photo below). You press the gauge into a wet layer of finish and read how thick the wet layer is. Then you calculate how thick the dry layer will be. For that, you must know the percentage of solids in the coating. The percentage of solids is also the percentage of wet thickness that will become dry thickness. In other words, if the wet coating is 4 mils thick and the material is 25% solids, then the dry film will be 25% of the 4-mil wet coat, or 1 mil dry. If it is a 100% solids coating, then 4 mils wet will become 4 mils dry.

There are three problems with this method. The first is that you must have a wet film thickness gauge, and they are not at all common. The second is that you must test the wet finish in an area that does not show, because the testing process leaves marks in the wet finish that do not come out. And finally, you must know the solids content of the finish. There must be an easier way.

I am reminded of the old story about a woman who gets onto a bus and says to the man beside her, "Could you tell me when to get off for Elm Street?" The man answers, "No problem. Just watch me and get off the stop before I do." That pretty much illustrates the way most experienced finishers tell whether a finish is thick enough to rub. They learned when to stop sanding by having sanded through on a previous finish, or more likely, on many previous finishes.

I suspect that this "learn from your own past mistakes" method is probably the best way to do it. Take some of those scrap wood samples you used to test out finishes, look at how thick the finish appears to be, and remember how many coats you put on and how thick each coat was. With that firmly in mind, start sanding and see how much you can sand before you sand through. And while you are at it, take note of how much easier it is to sand through on the edge than in the center. Sometimes experience is the best teacher.

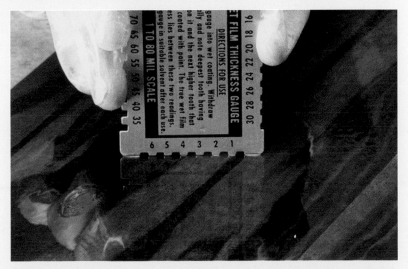

A wet film thickness gauge is used to calculate the thickness of the wet finish. From that measurement, you can calculate the thickness of the dry finish.

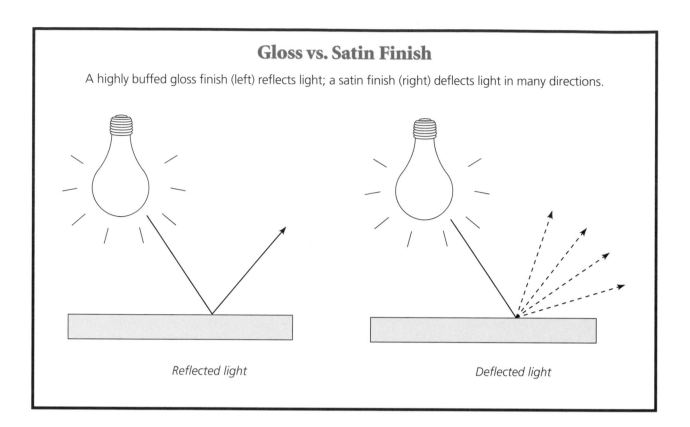

Gloss vs. Satin Finish

A highly buffed gloss finish (left) reflects light; a satin finish (right) deflects light in many directions.

Reflected light   *Deflected light*

I bought satin varnish for a pair of small tables I built. Even though I used the same can of varnish, the first one came out much glossier than the second. They were both sanded to the same grit and have the same number of coats. What gives?

It sounds like you did not stir the flatting agent into the varnish. Satin and matte coatings generally contain flatting agent that settles to the bottom of the can. When you open a new can of finish, run a stirring stick along the bottom of the can and you are likely to have a glob of whitish, hazy material on the end of it. This is the flatting agent, and you need to stir it uniformly throughout the varnish before you use it. If you do not, the first half of the can will be too shiny, and the second half too dull.

deflects more. In simple terms, the more light that is reflected, the shinier a finish looks, and the more light that is deflected, the flatter or duller a finish looks.

You can actually see the scratch pattern in a satin-rubbed finish, but not in a gloss finish. This is not a flaw in the process, but merely a characteristic of a rubbed surface. A rubbed satin finish will even look different depending on the angle from which it is viewed. If you look down the length of the scratches, they will appear less pronounced than if you sight across them. This is why finishers try to rub low-luster finishes in the direction of the grain. It makes the scratches less obvious without making the surface glossier.

Sheen

Sheen is the term we use to describe gloss. A higher sheen is shinier, or glossier, and a lower sheen is less shiny. The sheen of a finish is measured by the percentage of light that is reflected off the surface when viewed at a certain angle. The viewing is done by machines, which are somewhat less subjective than the human eye. The machine projects a measured amount of light at the surface at a given angle, then reads the amount that is reflected, reporting a percentage and an angle degree. A typical satin sheen callout might be: 35% sheen at 45°. Each manufacturer has his or her own idea of what constitutes matte, satin, semi-gloss, and gloss, but, as a general rule, matte usually ranges from 0% to 20%, satins run up to about 35%, semi-gloss to about 75%, and gloss may range all the way to 98%. It is virtually impossible to create 100% sheen, and you certainly can't go any higher than that.

Rubbing a finish creates an even pattern of scratches in it. Larger scratches make a duller finish, and finer scratches make a glossier finish. You can always rub a gloss finish down to satin by adding a coarser scratch pattern, but you can't always rub a satin finish to gloss. The reason is that lower-luster finishes, those that say "matte" or "satin" on the can, contain very finely ground inert particles called flatting agent. These small bits of powdered mineral become part of the surface of the dried material, making it slightly rough to our sight, but not rough to the touch. If we cut through these flatting particles with an abrasive, it may make the surface more level (and thus appear a bit glossier), but the flatting particles will still deflect instead of reflect light and keep the look of a satin finish. Therefore, it is best to start with a finish that is very close to the one you want to end up with after rubbing.

Unfortunately, if the finish is thick enough and contains enough flatting agent, it can start to become slightly cloudy. To get a really clear, thick finish, I prefer to build up with layers of gloss to avoid any cloudiness. Once it is as thick as I need it to be, I can rub it down to satin, or add just one or two coats of satin at the end.

Dried Satin Finish with Flatting Particles

In a dried satin finish, small bits of powdered mineral (flatting particles) deflect light whether or not the surface is leveled by rubbing.

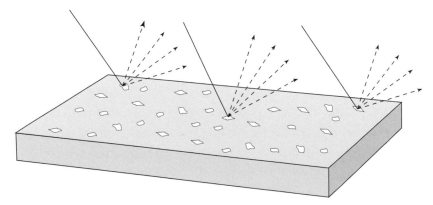

I put what I thought was gloss varnish on a library table, but I had accidentally bought satin. Is there a way to rub it to gloss?

It will become shinier if you polish it, closer to a semi-gloss, but will not be completely gloss. There is a limit to how glossy you can polish satin because satin coatings contain flatting agent. While you can get the surface flatter, hence glossier, you cannot remove the flatting agent from the dried coating. Rub it as you would a gloss finish, top it off with a glazing compound or swirl-mark remover, and you'll probably be happy with the results.

Rubbing and Polishing Materials

The business of rubbing is done by abrasives, which are minerals, or by steel wool (which, when you think about it, is also a mineral). You can buy the mineral in powdered form or premixed into a liquid compound or paste slurry. We generally talk about "rubbing to satin" and "polishing to gloss" because polishing compounds are a smaller size abrasive than rubbing compounds.

Powders

The old-timers in the world of finishing remember when all rubbing materials came in boxes and bags instead of cans and bottles. It is still possible to buy these powdered abrasives today, although they are getting scarce. The coarser powders are called pumice, and, true to their name, consist of ground-up pumice stone. They are graded on a one-letter scale, with F being the coarsest and FFFFF being the finest, similar to the steel-wool scale, which uses 0 to 00000. After the finest pumice, you graduate to rottenstone, a grayish powder that will yield a gloss finish.

If you want to use pumice and rottenstone, start by making a slurry of your chosen mineral and liquid. Pumice is usually added to mineral oil, which is sometimes cut with a little mineral spirits to make it thinner. With rottenstone you generally use water, perhaps with a bit of soap in it for more slip. Load a soft absorbent cloth pad or felt block with mineral oil, sprinkle a bit of pumice onto it, then have at it. The direction you rub is important only on the last grit you will use, since each graduation will, in theory at least, remove all previous scratches. As the pad stops cutting, add more pumice. If it starts to dry out or get too crusty, add oil and/or thinners.

Some finishers add finer and finer grits to one pad in the belief that the pumice breaks down to smaller particles with use. The more conscientious, however, carefully wipe off the wood surface and use a new clean pad for each successive grit. An intermediary wipe-down also lets you see your progress, because it is impossible to tell what's happening when you have a finish with the slurry on the top. You can keep going to finer grits until the finish is to your liking, or until you are too exhausted to care. If you are aiming for gloss, rottenstone will be your last step after the finest pumice. I like to store pumice and rottenstone in lidded salt shakers. It makes it easy to apply and keeps moisture out during storage.

Premixed Compounds

You are bound to find purists who swear by their own homemade pumice slurries. However, in my opinion, the premixed rubbing and polishing compounds are every bit as good and easier to use than anything you are likely to mix on your own.

At any good auto parts store you will find many brands of rubbing and polishing compounds. Some will simply be divided into rubbing and polishing, while others will have a range of abrasive grades from coarse to ultra fine. They all work, so find a set that feels right, smells decent, and is priced for your budget. My current favorites are shown in the photo at right, but that is strictly a matter of personal taste, and I have used many brands with equal success.

For a Satin Finish

The first step after the finish has cured sufficiently is a gentle sanding operation. To remove any nibs or unevenness in the surface, scuff-sand lightly with 400-grit self-lubricating sandpaper. Sand with the grain whenever possible. In the event that you sand through on an edge, it is easier to touch up if the flaw is with the grain. This operation will enhance any defects in seconds and give you feedback on how far you must sand (see the photo on p. 168). Follow up with 600-grit self-

lubricating paper or with wet/dry lubricated with mineral spirits or soapy water.

Once the surface is flat and sanded, you could move on to a rubbing compound or pumice. However, I prefer to rub with steel wool and paste wax. The steel wool leaves soft, U-shaped scratches, and the wax acts as a rubbing lubricant. If you prefer not to wax, substitute a mild soap in water (such as Murphy's Oil soap) wherever I talk about wax, and eliminate the dewaxing step at the end. On dark, open-pore finishes, light-colored paste wax can leave a whitish residue in the pores. For these, use a dark paste wax, or simply use dark wax shoe polish thinned with mineral spirits.

Wipe off any sanding dust or soap residue with a damp rag. Dip a piece of

You can buy rubbing abrasives in powdered form or as premixed compounds. Storing pumice and rotten-stone in lidded salt shakers makes them easier to dispense and keeps the mineral dry.

As you start to sand, any defects, like the orange peel on the left, will be enhanced. Continue to sand until the surface is flat, as in the area on the right.

What are the best lubricants to use when wet sanding?

It's a matter of personal taste. I have used plain water, soapy water, naphtha, mineral spirits, mineral oil, potassium oleate soap (wool wax), and even diluted paste wax all with good results. Each feels different, so you have to try them.

If you use an oil, wax, or soap, make sure you remove any film residue before recoating with more finish or you could have delamination problems. Clean oil or wax with naphtha. Clean off soap or wool wax using warm water with just a bit of ammonia added. Naphtha and mineral spirits need only be wiped with a clean, dry cloth.

0000 or 00000 steel wool into the wax and quickly wipe down the surface from end to end going with the grain to spread the wax. Start with the ends, first using short strokes, going with the grain (see the drawing on the facing page). That ensures that you don't miss the ends and lets you focus on carefully rubbing the edges without cutting through the finish. Keep your hand flat and avoid rolling the steel wool over the edge, which will cut through the finish on sharp edges. You can also use a flat foam pad to back up the steel wool if you prefer.

Rubbing Out a Satin Finish

1 End treatment—do once.

2 Dip the steel wool in paste wax and rub the surface end to end with the grain.

3 Overlap passes on long strokes and repeat the process six times.

When the edges are done, go to long strokes, from end to end. Overlap each pass and cover the entire board at least six times to ensure a uniform pattern. Try to keep the long strokes parallel and avoid curved swings that leave long, arched scratches. Don't be afraid to apply some pressure during this operation; after all, this is the aerobic part of this complete finishing sequence. To check your progress, squeegee an area with your thumb or a rubber pad, or simply wipe an area dry. When the surface looks and feels good, stop. Rubbing too much will only cause you to cut through the finish.

Wipe off as much wax as you can using a clean cloth or paper towels. You'll notice that even though you wipe aggressively, there is still enough wax left on the surface to smear when you rub it with your thumb. For a smear-free finish, you need to remove more wax. Sprinkle water on the surface (it should bead up), and with a clean, new steel-wool pad, repeat the rub pattern once or twice, but this time, do it very lightly, applying no pressure

Removing Wax

1 To remove wax used as a rubbing lubricant, first sprinkle water on the finish. The wax causes the water to bead up.

2 Now rub lightly with a clean pad.

3 When you are done, the pad should be coated with wax.

beyond the weight of your hand. Take a look at the pad. It should be coated with wax, and the top of the piece should be clean and smudge free. Wipe off any remaining water with a clean cloth or towel and step back and admire your work.

This satin finish is by far my favorite type of rubbed finish. It looks good, feels great, and works well with open-pore woods. Besides, it hides a multitude of minor finish defects—not that any of us have flaws in our finishes, mind you.

For a Gloss Finish

To get a high shine, start with a gloss, filled-pore finish that is completely cured. Open-pore finishes do not look good in gloss because the pores fill with rubbing compound. Make sure that the finish is thick enough and dry enough to rub. A finish that is not completely cured is harder to rub and will not get as shiny. The longer you wait to rub it out, the easier it will be to buff to high gloss. The cure times listed in the chart on the facing page are absolute minimums, and you would do well to double them if you can spare the time.

Minimum Cure Time for Rubbing

Finish	Cure time for satin rub	Cure time for gloss rub
Shellac	3 days	3 weeks
Sprayed lacquer	3 days	3 weeks
Brushing lacquer	7 days	1 month
Oil varnish, oil-based polyurethane	7 days	1 month
Waterborne coatings	7 days	1 month
Catalyzed lacquer, conversion varnish	2 days	7 days

Note: Cure times start one day after the final coat has been applied.

Go through the same sanding steps as for a satin rub, starting by scuff-sanding with 400-grit self-lubricating paper. Sand with the grain for this step, but after the 400-grit step, it does not matter what direction you sand, since you will soon be removing all of the scratches anyway. Continue on to 600-grit, but don't stop there; for gloss you need to move on to 1200- then 1500-grit paper. Wipe off the slurry when you are finished sanding. The surface should look completely uniform, with the appearance of brushed brass.

Make a pad of a soft cotton cloth dampened with water, dip it into the rubbing compound, and start rubbing. The direction does not matter, since you will be removing any visible scratches. I generally work in small circles in a pattern similar to what I use for French polishing (see the drawing on p. 126). When the sanding scratches are gone, move on to polishing compound with a new pad and

After building a new coffee table for the living room, I finished it in gloss varnish. The top is walnut, which I left unfilled so the pores show. It is shiny, but there are some bits of dust or dirt in the top that make it feel coarse. Can I rub these out and still keep the gloss?

Rubbing an open-pore gloss finish is almost always a bad idea. The process of rubbing to gloss will most likely leave compound packed into the pores. If the compound dries white, as most do, it will show badly. Even if you use a dark compound, or rottenstone, which is gray, the pores will be filled with a flat, chalky material instead of the gloss you started with. Gloss works best with filled pores and needs to be buffed.

You can rub the table down to satin with a dark wax, and it will look passable if not great. The dried dark wax that collects in the pores will leave them close to the sheen of the rubbed satin. But that will leave your table satin instead of the gloss you wanted.

FINISHING TALES

"Houston, We Have Liftoff..."

Mack was both creative and lazy, so he was forever coming up with unorthodox ways of making jobs go faster or easier. On rare occasions, his "inventions" worked. His penchant for reading science fiction during lunch break combined with his often impractical "solutions" earned him the affectionate nickname "Space Cadet."

One afternoon our boss, Brian, asked him to buff out a veneered, mahogany dining-room tabletop. It had been in the shop for weeks while we stripped, stained, filled, and glazed it to get it looking right. Now, after sitting around curing, the gloss lacquer was ready to be buffed. It was late afternoon when Mack finished all the sanding operations, and by then his fertile mind was working overtime. Since we did mostly satin finishes, the boss had never sprung for a power buffer and Mack was dreading polishing that huge table by hand.

The next day, he came in beaming. Tucked under his arm was a greasy, right-angle auto-motive body grinder cleverly retrofitted with a lamb's wool buffing pad. He was going to let the machine do the work. What none of us knew at the time was that a grinder spins considerably faster than a buffer. Mack slathered rubbing compound onto the table, plugged in his "helper," and set to work. The whirling pad tore through that buffing job lickety-split, flinging rubbing compound in a wide circle around the shop. But as Mack moved it toward the edge of the table, he must have tilted it the wrong way. The spinning pad burned right through the finish all along the edge, leaving an ugly light patch of raw wood where the dark glazed finish had been.

I suppose the shock of seeing what he had done to the finish must have unnerved him, because just then, he relaxed his grip on the grinder just a bit too much. In a split second, the spinning wool pad caught the corner of the table, wrenched the grinder from his hands, and sent it skittering across the top of the table, its heavy metal body bumping fresh dents into the shiny mahogany surface.

With flawless timing, Brian chose just that moment to emerge from his office. He stared in shock for a moment, then bellowed across the room, "What the heck do you think you're doing?" David, one of the new employees, broke the ensuing silence with a question. "Adding distress marks to the top?" he quipped. Brian was not amused.

It took us six weeks to strip the table, steam up the dents, reapply the finish, and wait for it to cure. The day before it was due to be polished, Brian walked in and deposited a fairly large box on Mack's workbench. Inside was a brand new buffer, complete with a state-of-the-art "safety" buffing head made of thick foam. With great fanfare, Brian handed Mack the instructions for using the buffer and said, loud enough for the whole shop to hear, "Try reading THIS during your lunch hour today."

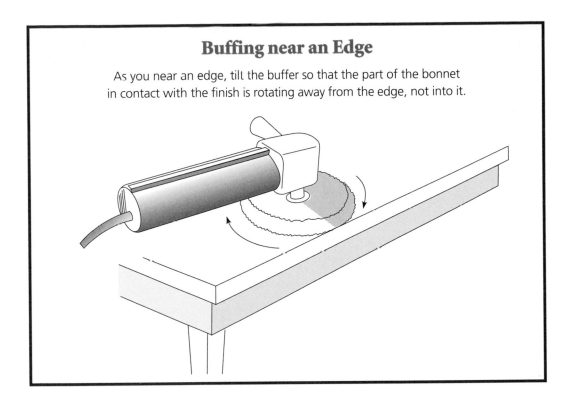

Buffing near an Edge

As you near an edge, tilt the buffer so that the part of the bonnet in contact with the finish is rotating away from the edge, not into it.

rub until all the scratches from the rubbing compound are gone. Periodically, wipe off the compound and take a look at the surface. It should be shiny enough to see yourself in—and you'll probably look exhausted.

As you may have noticed, most of the shining up took place right before the compound dried completely on the surface. This is the point when most of the lubricant has flashed off, and the concentration of abrasive grit on the pad is highest. Be careful, though; it is also the stage that the greatest amount of heat is created, and on a particularly heat-sensitive finish, you could soften the finish enough to burn through it.

Buff off any compound residue with a clean, soft cloth. Follow up with a coat of swirl-mark remover or "glazing liquid,"

such as Meguiar's #7, which is available in auto stores. Wipe it on and buff it off to leave the finish just a tad shinier.

Machine Polishing

Virtually every step of a gloss finish can be done faster (and just as well) with machines. However, if you plan to wet-sand using water or flammable solvents, stick to air-powered sanders instead of electric ones. Otherwise, the process is the same—go through a succession of sanding grits, then on to rubbing and finally polishing compound using a power buffer.

Like all power tools, buffers give you the ability to do more work and make worse mistakes faster. Remember all those places in the book that I told you to practice the finish on scrap? Well, take some

You can clean a lamb's wool bonnet by running it against the sharp edge of a hardwood stick clamped in a vise.

of those finished pieces of scrap and practice buffing the finish on them. In any case, here are some tips for working with a power buffer.

- Start the machine with the bonnet already on the surface, not up in the air.

- Don't press down—let only the weight of the machine do the work.

- Keep the buffer moving while it is running.

- Lift the buffer off the surface while it is still running.

- Keep only half the bonnet in contact with the finish at a time.

- As you near an edge, tilt the buffer so that the part of the bonnet in contact with the finish is rotating away from the edge, not into it.

As if to prove that buffing direction is not an issue, power buffers are orbital; they spin around a central point. There are special buffing compounds available for use with machines, but frankly, you can get excellent results with those designed for hand rubbing as well. Most auto store compounds are designed to work well with either hand or machine rubbing. Again, the sequence of rubbing is the same—polish with a succession of finer-grit compounds, cleaning or replacing the bonnet with each new grit. To clean the buff between grits, run it lightly across the edge of a sharpened stick held firmly in a vise, as shown in the photo above. The final step is a very light pass with a completely clean, soft head, then a follow-up with a hand-applied coat of swirl-mark remover.

Resources

I have made a point of trying to stick to materials that you can buy at the local paint, hardware, and home store. There are a few exceptions, though, so here are some sources for materials that are not easily available. Those listed below sell most of these items direct (mail order).

For dyes, shellac flakes, brushes, and touchup supplies:

Homestead Finishing Products
11929 Abbey Road Unit G
Cleveland, OH 44133-2677
(440) 582-8929
FAX (800) 286-0941

Woodworker's Supply
1108 N. Glenn Rd.
Casper, WY 82601
(800) 645-9292
FAX (800) 853-9663

Woodcraft
210 Wood County Industrial Park
Parkersburg, WV 26102-1686
(800) 225-1153
FAX (304) 428-8271
www.woodcraft.com

Lee Valley & Veritas
PO Box 1780
Ogdensburg, NY 13669-9973
(800) 871-8158
FAX (800) 513-7885
www.leevalley.com

Mohawk Finishing Products
4715 State Hwy. 30
Amsterdam, NY 12010-7417
(800) 545-0047
FAX (800) 721-1545

And for an unusually fine selection of specialty brushes:

Pearl Paint
308 Canal St.
New York, NY 10013
(800) 221-6845
FAX (800) PEARL-91
www.pearlpaint.com

Glossary

The biggest problem with understanding finishing is that the materials we use are formulated by chemists, and chemists speak a different language than the rest of us. They talk about esters, ketones, polyols, and resin weights, and we come away with the distinct impression that if they'd only stick to English, life would be much easier. Of course, we woodworkers are just as bad. Try talking to non-woodworkers about dadoes, mortises, raised panels, and chamfers and see how quickly their eyes glaze over.

Since it doesn't look as if the chemists are going to change, I guess it's up to us to learn their language. Here's a guide to some of the most common chemical terms you may encounter as a wood finisher. Many of these terms are discussed more fully in the text; for page references, please consult the Index (pp. 180-183).

Aniline dyes Technically, a large class of synthetic dyes (soluble colorants), made from intermediates based upon anilines. In woodworking, the term is used generically to cover all soluble wood dyes, even if they are not specifically anilines.

Asphaltum The paint industry's term for gilsonite ground in oil. Asphaltum makes an interesting wood stain and glaze when it is diluted with mineral spirits.

Binder The portion of the liquid part of a coating that does not evaporate. The binder is generally referred to as the resin.

Blush The whitish, cloudlike haze that occurs in fast-drying finishes, especially lacquer, when it is sprayed in very humid conditions. Blush is most often due to moisture (water vapor) trapped in the film or to bits of resin precipitating out of solution.

Burning in The process of melting lacquer or shellac sticks by touching them with a heated knife and using the resulting liquid to fill small voids in a finish.

Burnish To close off or collapse wood pores by rubbing with a dull object. Sanding grit that gets dull through use will burnish wood grain rather than cut through it.

Catalyst Anything that speeds up a chemical reaction without being used up by it. Most finish catalysts are chemicals (e.g., the heavy metals used to speed up linseed oil's drying time), but even sunlight can act as a catalyst.

Catalyzed lacquers A term used for a variety of crosslinking spray coatings and, more specifically, for those lacquers whose cure is initiated by an acid.

Colorant The portion of a stain that actually imparts the color. Liquid stain consists of colorant added to a vehicle.

Combustible Any material that will ignite (or whose vapors will ignite) at some temperature. *See also* Flammable. Nonflammable.

Conversion varnish A two-part crosslinking spray coating. The term is often used interchangeably with catalyzed lacquer.

Crosslinked finishes This term includes all reactive, conversion, and catalyzed finishes and refers to a finish that forms larger polymers (molecules) during its curing time after it has been applied to the wood.

Danish oil finish The general term for any of the various wipe-on finishes, usually consisting of some drying oil (such as tung or linseed) thinned with mineral spirits and bolstered with a small amount of resin (usually alkyd).

Doping in The process of filling voids in a finish by adding drops of the same finish, then leveling the dried material. It is also called "kootching."

Dyes Soluble colorants used to make stains that do not scatter light but absorb certain wavelengths and transmit others. Because they dissolve in their solvent, dyes afford deep, translucent color to stains and wood. *See also* Pigments.

Evaporative finishes Coatings (also called solvent-release finishes) that form films by the evaporation of their volatile component, with no polymerization or other crosslinking taking place during drying. Consequently, they can be redissolved by their solvent at any time, even long after cure. Some examples are shellac and lacquer.

Filler A thick dispersion of ground pigment, silica, talc, and/or other materials used to fill the large pores in coarse-grained woods. Also called pore filler, it is designed so that once dry, it will not shrink under subsequent coats of finish.

Finish Any protective coating applied as a liquid or gel.

Flammable Indicating a substance whose flash point is below 100°F. *See also* Combustible.

Flash point The lowest temperature at which a liquid or its vapors will ignite in the presence of a flame or spark.

French polish Originally, French polish was a shellac and alcohol mixture designed to be applied by hand with a cloth pad to produce a high-gloss finish. In current use, the term refers to both the material and the process of application.

Gloss The measure of the percentage of light a surface reflects. With finishes, gloss is measured by shining light on the surface at a particular angle and reading the reflected amount at the complementary angle. Both the percentage of reflected light and angle are called out. A typical reading might be "35 sheen at 60°," meaning that 35% of the shone light was reflected at a 60° angle.

Japan colors Pigments ground in boiled linseed oil or some other oil to which Japan driers have been added. These opaque colorants handle like oil colors but dry faster.

Japan driers Heavy metal salts or soaps added to drying oils in order to speed up the cure. Their action is a true catalytic one. They initiate or speed polymerization without changing chemically or becoming part of the molecule. The metals remain trapped in the matrix of the dried film.

Lacquer Any film-forming finish that dries by solvent evaporation alone. (The term "catalyzed lacquer" is an oxymoron.)

Linseed oil A reactive drying oil derived from the seeds of the flax plant. Many oil stains and varnishes are made from linseed oil.

Lower explosive limit (LEL) The minimum amount of a substance that must be in the air for it to be able to explode or ignite. It is expressed as a volume percentage in air.

Matte A degree of sheen below satin and above dead flat, although it is sometimes used as a synonym for dead flat.

Metamerism The phenomenon exhibited by a pair of colors that match under one set of lighting conditions but not under a different set.

Mineral spirits Nonflammable but combustible petroleum distillates that are used as solvents and diluents for a variety of coatings, especially oil-based coatings.

Naphtha A common flammable solvent for oil-based coatings and stains consisting of aromatic and/or aliphatic hydrocarbons. Hi-flash naphtha is generally aromatic; VM&P (varnish maker's and painter's) naphtha is mostly aliphatic.

Noncombustible That which will not ignite at any temperature.

Nonflammable That which will not ignite below 100°F. A substance can be both combustible and non-flammable.

Oil-based finish More or less a synonym for oil varnish.

Oil varnish Any air-drying varnish based on or containing drying oils as the primary film former.

Orange peel A finish flaw in sprayed finishes, where the coating does not lay out smoothly but takes on the texture of the skin of an orange. It is usually caused by spraying material that is too thick or poorly atomized.

Overspray A dry, pebbly texture caused when sprayed finish dries in the air before hitting the wood. The droplets of finish adhere as dried particles rather than flowing out as a liquid.

Oxalic acid A crystalline powder that mixes with water to form a bleach for wood. It is especially effective at removing stains caused by the contact of iron with woods high in tannin. In spite of the fact that it occurs naturally in rhubarb and spinach, it is both toxic and irritating.

Padding lacquer Premixed, commercially made French polish. It frequently contains resins other than just shellac along with solvents other than alcohol.

Permissible exposure level (PEL) *See* Threshold limit value.

Pickling stains Pigmented wiping stains based on white or pastel colors. Left in grain, carvings, and corners, they are used to create limed and pickled finishes.

Pigmented oil stains Oil-based stains that use pigments (as opposed to dyes) as their coloring agent.

Pigments In paint formulator's parlance, pigment is any dry particulate mineral added to coatings, stains, fillers, etc. The pigment can be colorless, like the fine silica added to clear coatings to reduce gloss, or it can be highly colored, like the pigments ground into oil to make Japan colors and paint. Although all pigments are opaque, their size and the amount added to the finish control their power to make the coating itself opaque. *See also* Dyes.

Polyurethane The name used for a wide variety of resins used in both oil and waterborne coatings. They add toughness, durability, and heat resistance to coatings.

Pore filler *See* Filler.

Primer A barrier or coupling coat used to seal a substrate or to increase adhesion between the substrate and the finish coats. Primer is simply colored opaque sealer.

Pumice A volcanic rock. Finely ground pumice is used as a rubbing compound for satin finishes or as the first abrasive for gloss finishes.

Putty A thick mixture of binder, solvent, and colored or neutral pigment used to fill defects and voids in raw wood prior to finishing. Not to be confused with pore filler, which is essentially a thinner version of the same basic ingredients.

Reactive finishes Finishes (also called thermoset finishes) that form a film by some means other than simply solvent evaporation, most commonly by polymerization. All oil-based varnishes and crosslinked or catalyzed coatings are reactive.

Relative humidity A measure of the amount of moisture in the air, expressed as a percentage of the maximum amount of moisture the air is capable of holding at that temperature. Warm air can hold more water vapor than cool air.

Resin The general term for any polymer or monomer used as the binder or film former in a coating.

Satin A degree of finish sheen below semi-gloss and above eggshell or matte.

Scuff sanding A very light, quick sanding operation designed to remove minor roughness from wood or a coat of finish. Scuff sanding is done with very little pressure and fine (220-grit or finer) sandpaper.

Sealer A barrier or coupling coat of finish designed to seal the substrate and/or increase adhesion of the topcoat. Sealer is the clear version of primer. Sanding sealer contains added pigments, usually stearates, to make it build faster and sand more easily.

Seedlac A form of shellac obtained from the original crude product. *See also* Shellac.

Sheen The term used to describe gloss. A higher sheen is shinier, or glossier, and a lower sheen is less shiny. The sheen of a finish is measured by the percentage of light that is reflected off the surface when viewed at a certain angle.

Shellac The alcohol-soluble resin derived from the natural secretions of the female of the insect *Laccifer lacca*. Shellac has a long history in finishing, and still enjoys prominence as an effective sealer and the only resin of true French polish. There are many grades and refinements of shellac, from the crudest seedlac to dewaxed Kusmi aghani flakes.

Solvent A liquid capable of dissolving a resin or solid, and more broadly, the volatile portion of a coating mixture.

Solvent-release finishes *See* Evaporative finishes.

Spar varnish Any oil-based varnish designed for exterior use. Traditional spar varnish is made from tung oil and phenolic resin, which is flexible enough to allow wood movement, and has natural UV resistance.

Stain Any liquid or gel that adds color when it is applied to raw wood.

Stearated Containing zinc stearate, magnesium stearate, or aluminum stearate. Stearates are soft, powdery soaps used both as a bodying agent in sanding sealer and as an anti-clogging lubricant layer on stearated sandpaper.

Thermoplastic finishes Finishes that will resoften with the addition of heat, i.e., solvent-release finishes.

Threshold limit value (TLV) The maximum allowable exposure in an 8-hour period to a hazardous substance, measured in parts per million (ppm). Another term for TLV is PEL (permissible exposure level).

Universal tinting colors (UTCs) Pigments ground in a solvent or medium designed to be compatible with a wide range of coating resins and solvents, including both water-based and oil-based coatings.

Varnish At various times, the term varnish implied only clear coatings, only brushed coatings, or only oil-based coatings. It is currently used as a general term for finish. Some folks differentiate by calling reactive finishes varnish and evaporative finishes lacquer.

Vehicle The liquid portion of a stain or coating in which solid particles, like pigment, are suspended. Vehicles can be either solvents or resins or both.

Viscosity The thickness of a liquid. High-viscosity liquids are thick, low-viscosity liquids are thin.

Water-based oil stains Emulsions of an oil-based stain in water, water-based oil stains act like oil-based stains but have lower volatile organic compound (VOC) levels.

Water-based pigmented stains Dispersions of pigment in water with a compatible resin binder (usually acrylic) and the necessary solvents, surfactants, and other additives.

Wiping stain Any easy-to-use or thickened stain, but more commonly a thickened pigmented oil stain.

Witness line The faint line that appears when you sand or buff through one coat of a polymerized finish into a previous layer.

Index

A

Alcohol, types of, 14
Ammonia, rinse with, 56
Application:
    with abrasives, 23
    brushed, finish for, 8
    of fillers, 110–15
    of lacquer, 25, 131, 143–44
    of oil finishes, 122–24
    paper towels for, 22–23
    of polyurethane, 128–31
    rags for, 22–23, 123–124, 126
    of shellac, 22, 124–27, 131, 143
    sprayed, finish for, 8
    of stain, 93–94
    of varnishes, 124, 128–31, 143–44
    of waterborne finish, 131–32, 145
    See also Brushes. Spray guns.
Ash:
    filler for, 109, 110
    pigment staining, 94
Asphaltum:
    defined, 176
    as stain, 95

B

Bar tops, finish for, 8, 13, 17
Beams, ceiling, finish for, 18
Benches, outdoor, finish for, 15
Binder, defined, 176
Biological hazards: *See* Safety.
Bleaches:
    laundry, 58–59
    wood, 59, 60–61
Blush:
    defined, 176
    pictured, 119, 144
Boats, finish for, 15
Bookcases, finish for, 9
Boxes:
    finish for, 11, 12, 14
    jewelry, finish for, 9
Brushes:
    care of, 29–31
    foam, 24–25
    types of, 26–29
    using, 128–32

Buffing: *See* Rubbing out.
Burning in:
    defined, 176
    process of, 150–55
Burnish, defined, 176

C

Cabinets, finish for, 13
Catalyst, defined, 176
Chairs:
    finish for, 12
    outdoor, finish for, 8, 15
Chatoyance:
    defined, 10
    finishes for, 10
Cherry:
    conditioner for, 83
    sealer for, 101
Cocobolo, sealer for, 104
Colorant, defined, 78, 176
Colors:
    altering, with dye, 88–89
    artist's oil, defined, 91
    Japan, defined, 91, 177
    layered, 92
    metamerism with, 81
    for sealer, 109–10
    universal tinting, defined, 91, 179
    See also Pigments.
Combustible, defined, 176
Countertops, finish for, 17
Cradles, finish for, 14
Cribs, finish for, 14
Crosslinked finishes, defined, 176
Cure times:
    and finish coat, 118
    and humidity, 119
    for rubbing out, 171
    and solvents, 129
    and temperature, 119

D

Dalbergia spp., sealer for, 104–105
Danish oil: *See* Oil finishes.
Dents, repairing, 62–64, 107
Doors, exterior, finish for, 15
Doping in:
    defined, 177
    process of, 150, 151

Drawers, finish for, 11
Dry brushing, process of, 97–100
Dyes:
    aniline, defined, 176
    concentrates, 87
    defined, 78, 177
    and filler, 108
    removing, 90
    sealer for, 104, 105, 107
    solvents for, 86–87
    under stain, 92, 94
    tinting with, 88
    See also Stains.

E

Ebonizing, process of, 86
End grain, preparing, 91, 103, 105–106
Evaporative finishes, defined, 3–5, 177
Explosion: *See* Safety.
Eye protection, types of, 21, 22

F

Figure, finish for, 85
Fillers:
    clear, applying, 114–16
    defined, 65, 101, 177
    and dye, 108
    dye-accepting, 116
    need for, 111
    oil-based, 109–10
        applying, 110–14
    over sealer, 109
    and stains, 108
    uses of, 108–109
    waterborne, applying, 114–15
Filters, using, 40
Finish:
    choosing, 8–19
    defined, 2–3, 177
Finishing room, requirements for, 117–19
Fire: *See* Safety.
Fisheye, sealer avoiding, 104, 105
Flammable, defined, 177
Flash point, defined, 177
Floors, finish for, 17
French polish:
    defined, 177
    method for, 126–27
    over polyurethane, 155

Furniture:
    high wear, finish for, 13, 17
    low-wear, finish for, 14
    moderate-wear, finish for, 10, 12, 14, 16
    outdoor, finish for, 15

G

Glazing, process of, 94–97
Gloss, defined, 177
Gloves, types of, 21
Gouges, repairing, 62–64, 107
Graining, and finish removal, 56

H

Heat, resistance to, 4, 5

J

Japan colors, defined, 91, 177
Japan driers, defined, 177

K

Knots, adding, 159

L

Lacquer:
    applying, 143
    blushing of, 119, 144
    brushes for, 26, 28
    brushing, applying, 131
    burn-in sticks of, 150–51, 155
    catalyzed
        applying, 143–44
        defined, 176
        problems with, 143
        qualities of, 8–9, 19
        sealer for, 103
    defined, 177
    filters for, 40
    finish over, 18
    and foam pads, 24
    mixing containers for, 42
    orange peel with, 144, 168
    padding, defined, 178
    problems with, 144
    qualities of, 9–10, 19
    rubbing out, cure time for, 171
    sealer under, 102–103, 104, 105, 106

shelf life of, 18
solvents for, 129
stripper for, 44, 46–47
tinting, 88
waterborne
    applying, 25
    with polyurethane, qualities of,
        17, 19
    qualities, 16, 19
Lauan, sealer for, 102
Lower explosive limit (LEL), defined, 6, 177

M

Mahogany:
    filler for, 101, 109
    layered finish for, 92
    pigment staining, 93
Mantels, finish for, 8
Material safety data sheets (MSDS),
        obtaining, 6
Matte, defined, 177
Metamerism, defined, 81, 177
Mineral spirits, defined, 177
Mixing containers, choosing, 42

N

Naphtha, defined, 178
Noncombustible, defined, 178
Nonflammable, defined, 178

O

Oak:
    filler for, 109, 110
    pigment staining, 93, 94
Odors, from finish, avoiding, 126
Oil finishes:
    applying, 122–24
    Danish
        creep with, 121
        defined, 177
        qualities of, 9, 19
    defined, 178
    hand-rubbed, 122
    linseed, defined, 177
    qualities of, 10–11, 19
    rub out of, cure time for, 171
    sandpapered on, 23
    sealer over, 107

shelf life of, 18
solvents for, 129
strippers for, 47, 51
vs. waterborne finishes, 17
See also Varnishes: oil.
Orange peel:
    defined, 178
    pictured, 144, 168
Overspray:
    defined, 178
    pictured, 144
Oxalic acid:
    defined, 178
    using, 59–60

P

Paint:
    brushes for, 26–27
    pads for, 24, 131–32
    strippers for, 47, 51
    thinned, as stain, 93
Permissible exposure level (PEL), defined,
        178
Pickling:
    process of, 97
    protection for, 16
Pigments:
    defined, 78, 178
    making, 92
    purchased, 90–92
    See also Colors. Stains.
Pine, sealer for, 102
Polish: See Rubbing out.
Polyurethane:
    applying, 128–31
    defined, 178
    French polish over, 155
    gel, qualities of, 12, 19
    rubbing out, cure time for, 171
    shelf life of, 18
    over shellac, 104
    solvents for, 129
    strippers for, 51
    varnish, qualities of, 12–13, 19
    waterborne
        and crosslinked lacquer, qualities of,
            17, 18, 19
        qualities of, 16–17, 19

Poplar:
  pigment staining, 93
  sealer for, 101, 102
Pore fillers: *See* Fillers.
Prefinishing:
  advantages of, 121
  defined, 117
  process of, 120–21
Primers:
  defined, 101, 106, 178
  using, 106–107
Pumice, defined, 178
Putty:
  defined, 178
  red-spot, 106–107
  types of, 64
  using, 65

R

Reactive finishes, defined, 4, 5, 178
Refinishing: *See* Shellac: reamalgamating.
      Stripping.
Relative humidity:
  defined, 178
  for finish application, 119
Repairs:
  of brittle finishes, 147–49
  of debris, 146–47
  of flexible finishes, 149
  of runs, 147, 149
  touchup for, 155–59
  of voids, 150–55
  of witness lines, 148, 161, 162
  See also Surface preparation.
Resin:
  defined, 179
  types of, 3
Respirators, types of, 21, 22
Rosewood:
  filler for, 109
  sealer for, 103, 104–105
Rubbing out:
  abrasives for, 166–67
  cure times for, 171
  defined, 160–61
  difficulty of, charted, 161

to gloss, 170–73
  lubricants for, 168
  with machines, 172, 173–74
  and open-pore finish, 170, 171
  to satin, 166–70
    vs. gloss, 162–65, 166

S

Safety:
  from biological hazards, 7
  equipment for, 20–22
  and explosions, 6–7
  and fire, 6
    with solvents, 6
  with strippers, 45
  with wax, 122
  See also Spray guns: booths for.
Sanding:
  blocks for, 72, 74
  importance of, 5
  schedule for, 66, 72–74
  scuff, defined, 179
  wet, 168
Sandpaper:
  grits of, 66–70, 75
  open-coat vs. closed, 71
  stearated, 71–72
  wet/dry, 72
Satin, defined, 179
Sealers:
  defined, 101, 179
  under filler, 109
  glue size as, 103, 105–106
  under lacquer, 102
  sanding, 101, 102
  shellac as, 103–104
  vinyl, 104–105
Seedlac, defined, 179
Sheen, defined, 165, 179
Shelf lives, of finishes, listed, 18
Shellac:
  applying, 22, 124–27, 131, 143
  brushes for, 26, 28
  defined, 179
  dewaxed, 104, 125
  finish over, 18

measuring, 40
  mixed, test for, 125
  mixing, 125, 141
  mixing containers for, 42
  as odor sealer, 126
  qualities of, 13–14, 15, 19
  reamalgamating, 44
  rubbing out, cure time for, 171
  as sealer, 102, 103–104, 105
  shelf life of, 18
  solvents for, 129
  stripper for, 44, 46–47
  tinting, 87, 88
  white primer, 107
  See also French polish.
Shelves, finish for, 12
Softwoods, conditioner for, 83
Solvent-release finishes, defined, 179
Solvents:
  defined, 179
  and finish types, 5
  for lacquer, 129
  mixing containers for, 42
  for oil-based finishes, 129
  protection against, 20–22
  for rinsing, 56
  for shellac, 129
  for varnish, 129
  for waterborne finishes, 129
  for wax, 129
  See also individual finishes.
Sources, listed, 175
Spray guns:
  aerosol substitute for, 133
  booths for, 134–37, 140
  filters for, 40, 41
  patterns with, 140–42, 145
  standard vs. HVLP, 35
  technique for, 142–45
  turntable for, 138–40
  types of, 32–37
  viscosity measures for, 41–42